WE MUST RUN THIS RACE

RICKY CLEMONS

PUBLISHED BY FIDELI PUBLISHING, INC.

ISBN: 978-1-955622-05-9

Published by

Fideli Publishing, Inc.
119 W. Morgan St.
Martinsville, IN 46151
www.FideliPublishing.com

Table of Contents

We Must Run this Race 1

God Allowed Only One Sperm to Fertilize an Egg 4

Life is Very Powerful 7

We Can Always be Thankful 9

Prayer Can 12

A Day to Rejoice 14

One Church Body 16

God Commands Us to Love Our Neighbors 18

If We Can 23

There are People Who Believe 24

It's Very Rare These Days 25

It Can Cause Our Hearts to Hurt 26

Jesus was the Greatest War Veteran 27

Addicted to Pulling the Trigger 29

Use Your 31

Our Minds can Drift Off In 33

Doesn't Mean Anything Good at All 36

Live For 38

Goes Down the Drain Like Water 40

It's Always Good 42

The Only Book 44

God Surely Knew What He was Doing 46

If the Lord Questions Us 48

In This World Today 50

O Lord, Help Me 51

Can Be Used For 53

We Have No Time to Waste 55

A Day Will Go On About Its Business 57

If We had to Work Our Way 59

Will Use the Name of the Lord 61

Is Too Much 62

We Christians are Supposed to 63

As We Get Closer and Closer 65

The Facts of Life 67

There is More and More of You, O Lord 69

Be In My 71

The Lord Can Show You and Me 72

Survival is Pretty Much About 75

Regretting Something 77

The Origin Of 79

Falsely Accused 82

If You are Living in Sin 84

Loneliest 85

With His Smooth Temptations 86

It's Not Always Easy To 88

There Won't Be 90

God's Blessings..92

No Matter How Much You Tell People.....................94

You Can't Always...95

Don't Want to Have Anything to do With 96

Anybody Can Be..98

It was You, Lord Jesus 100

Conspiracy is of the Devil 102

Will Pass Away One Day 104

Will Think of Ways..106

We Would Rather Look at and Talk About 108

Age Doesn't Matter..110

The Lord Can Open Doors 112

Can't Do More than What God Allows....................113

There is Nothing God Can't Do................................115

We Take a Chance with Our Lives 117

The Christian Life..119

Don't Come Close To..123

The Best Good News to Spread 125

Being Content is Being Rich In 127

O Lord, You Know...128

Many People...129

Perfect 132

The Church is Not Perfect 134

Going Through the Great Tribulation 136

A Real Man and a Real Woman...138

Will Suffer in Some Kind of Way 140

You Can Thank Jesus...142

It's Good to Keep Quiet 144

We Christians Shouldn't be Too Hard on Ourselves 145

It's a Miracle 148

Can Add Up to and Subtract From 149

Will See No Wrong..151

It Will Take 154

Real Life is Not Rehearsed..156

Even After I Mess Things Up 158

You're Supposed to Love Everybody..159

Talkers and Listeners...161

Do You Believe in Jesus Christ?..163

Don't Put Off...165

Working for the Lord...166

The Greatest Travel..167

We Must Run this Race

We must run this race of going through trials to win our prize of eternal life through Jesus Christ.

We must run this race of denying self and picking up our crosses to follow Jesus to win our prize of eternal life through Jesus Christ.

We must run this race of holding onto Jesus to win our prize of eternal life through Jesus Christ.

We must run this race of keeping our eyes on Jesus to win our prize of eternal life through Jesus Christ.

We must run this race of having faith in Jesus to win our prize of eternal life through Jesus Christ.

We must run this race of putting our trust in Jesus to win our prize of eternal life through Jesus Christ.

We must run this race of giving the glory and praise to Jesus to win our prize of eternal life through Jesus Christ.

We must run this race of giving Jesus all of our hearts to win our prize of eternal life through Jesus Christ.

We must run this race of keeping ourselves humble unto Jesus to win our prize of eternal life through Jesus Christ.

We must run this race of dressing modestly in modest apparel to win our prize of eternal life through Jesus Christ.

We must run this race of spreading the gospel of Jesus Christ to win our prize of eternal life through Jesus Christ.

We must run this race of winning souls to Jesus to win our prize of eternal life through Jesus Christ.

We must run this race of using our spiritual gifts to edify the church to win our prize of eternal life through Jesus Christ.

We must run this race of being a witness of Jesus to win our prize of eternal life through Jesus Christ.

We must run this race of giving testimonies about what Jesus brought us through to win our prize of eternal life through Jesus Christ.

We must run this race of not quenching the Holy Spirit to win our prize of eternal life through Jesus Christ.

We must run this race of having the fruit of the Holy Spirit to win our prize of eternal life through Jesus Christ.

We run this race of being filled with the Holy Spirit to win our prize of eternal life through Jesus Christ.

We must run this race of confessing and repenting of our sins unto Jesus to win our prize of eternal life through Jesus Christ.

We must run this race of being born again in the spirit to win our prize of eternal life through Jesus Christ.

We must run this race of loving Jesus and keeping His Commandments to win our prize of eternal life through Jesus Christ.

Must run this race of being saved in Jesus to win our prize of eternal life through Jesus Christ.

We must run this race of not being a friend to this sinful world to win our prize of eternal life through Jesus Christ.

We must run this race of being a peculiar people to win our prize of eternal life through Jesus Christ.

We must run this race of having hope in Jesus to win our prize of eternal life through Jesus Christ.

We must run this race of believing in Jesus to win our prize of eternal life through Jesus Christ.

We must run this race of living our lives unto Jesus to win our prize of eternal life through Jesus Christ.

We must run this race of standing up for Jesus to win our prize of eternal life through Jesus Christ.

We must run this race of giving up our lives for Jesus to win our prize of eternal life through Jesus Christ.

We must run this race of giving up everything that we have for Jesus' name sake to win our prize of eternal life through Jesus Christ.

This race is not for the swift or strong but for all who endure to cross over the finish line in Jesus Christ, who is the only One who can give us His grand prize of eternal life.

In this race that we must run, it doesn't matter to the Lord if we run fast or slow, as long as we cross over the finish line to get our prize of eternal life.

In this race that we must run, we will trip over problems and fall down into some discouragement for Jesus to pick us up and encourage us to keep on running this race.

In this race that we must run, there are no losers because we all are winners to cross over the finish line in Jesus Christ, who will give us eternal life if we don't give up in running this race no matter how many times we get spiritually bumped into with false doctrines and pretense.

We must run this race on the strait and narrow road and only look straight ahead with our eyes on Jesus shining bright in this dark, sinful world that wants us to drop out of this race as soon as problems come our way on every side of the strait and narrow road that we run our race on to get our grand prize of eternal life in Jesus Christ.

We must run this race that is for anyone who confesses and repents of their sins unto the Lord Jesus Christ, who is the beginning and the end of this race that we must run with our eyes stayed on Jesus.

God Allowed Only One Sperm to Fertilize an Egg

Out of millions of sperms, God allowed only one sperm to fertilize an egg that procreated you and me in our mothers' wombs.

God made us so wonderfully, even in procreation, whether we were born in wedlock or out of wedlock.

None of us is a mistake to God, the origin of all life.

There are people who believe that their child is a mistake, but a child can grow up in the Lord if the parents raise up their child loving the Lord.

Even if that child has a mental or physical defect, the Lord can still bless that child in ways that you and I just can't understand.

Out of millions of sperms, God allowed only one sperm to fertilize an egg that procreated you and me in our mothers' wombs and allowed us to be born out of that dark, closed-in womb.

When Jonah was in the belly of the whale, he was very aware of where he was, surrounded by darkness in a closed-in place for three days.

That must have seemed to be like an eternity to Jonah.

For nine long months, a baby is kept in the dark, closed-off place of the womb where the baby is not aware of what is going on.

God allowed you and me to exist from only one sperm out of millions of sperms that were not allowed to fertilize an egg because God chose you and me to be born and grow up in this world to love and obey Him who kept us safe in our mothers' wombs.

God allows only one you to be born, even if you have a twin or quadruplets coming out of your mother's womb.

There's no one else who will be exactly like you who was procreated from that one sperm fertilizing an egg in your mother's womb.

You were chosen by God to live in this world out of millions of sperms on the journey to get to an egg when only one sperm could fertilize your mother's egg to procreate you.

God allowed only one sperm to fertilize an egg without a doubt in your mother's womb, and it was destined to be you in your mother's womb.

God didn't make a mistake when He allowed only one sperm out of millions of sperms to fertilize an egg in the womb of the woman who became your mother.

The only mistake that is made is to kill life that is from God.

It's the devil who hates the life in a mother's womb, whether the baby is in wedlock or from rape or from incest.

Life is from God, no matter how the baby comes into this world.

God can bless a baby that is the result of rape or incest to grow up and love Him and keep His Commandments.

Even a baby born from rape or incest is no mistake to God, even though it can look like a mistake to you and me.

God had foreseen it to be the right thing to have allowed that one sperm to fertilize an egg that gave you and me life in our mothers' wombs.

We can read all the medical and technical information about procreation, but only God created the reproductive system, even in animals who also procreate.

God created a man and a woman wonderfully and gave Adam and Eve all that they needed to populate this world with human beings that were allowed to come into existence from only one sperm fertilizing an egg.

Before any scientist, surgeon or doctor, God had predestined to create the human body with a reproductive system that the angels marveled at and gathered all the information from God about the human body's reproductive system.

Out of millions of sperms, only one sperm fertilized an egg to procreate you with a different personality from billions of other people in this world.

There is only one you, and God didn't make a mistake to allow you to be born into this world.

God didn't allow those millions of other sperms to interrupt that one sperm and stop it from fertilizing an egg that procreated you and me in our mothers' wombs that belong to God.

God wonderfully made the reproductive system to procreate tiny human beings from only one sperm out of millions of sperms that God didn't allow to fertilize an egg in the womb of a woman.

No baby is born to be a mistake to God.

If that wasn't true, you and I would be a mistake to God while we are living in this world.

No baby is at fault for being in a woman's womb.

Even if it's a result of rape or incest, it's not too hard for God to bless that baby to grow up and make good achievements in life.

Out of millions of sperms, God allowed only one sperm to fertilize an egg to procreate a tiny human being who became you and me.

You and I have no right in the eyes of God to take anyone's life, but God has every right to take life away, even in the womb of a woman.

In the eyes of God, the right way to procreate is in wedlock, but the devil has been trying to destroy this since way back in the Garden of Eden.

If a woman gets pregnant with an incest baby or a rape baby and she gets an abortion, then only God can judge her, and God will do that fairly.

God loves life, no matter how a baby is procreated in a mother's womb that is not hard for God to bless.

Out of millions of sperms, God allowed only one sperm to fertilize an egg that procreated you and me with life from God, who has the right to give life and take it away for His reasons that are always right beyond our reasons that can be wrong.

Life is Very Powerful

Many people are blind and can't see, but they want to live every day in this world.

Many people are deaf and can't hear but they want to live every day in this world.

Life is very powerful for many people to want to live, regardless of the misfortunes that they have in life.

Many people are paralyzed and can't walk, but they want to live every day in this world.

Many people have no arms and no legs, but they want to live every day in this world.

Life is very powerful for many people who want to live, regardless of the bad things that happened to them in their lives.

Many people are sick and can't do anything for themselves, but they want to live every day in this world.

Many people are locked up in prison for life, but they still want to live every day in this world.

God created life to be very powerful for everyone to live doing His holy will.

Life is very powerful, regardless of many people taking their own lives because they think their lives are of no value and they don't want to live.

Life is very powerful for you and me to live again after we die for Jesus Christ to give us eternal life when He comes back again.

Many people are homeless and many people are poor, but they want to live in this world where life means hope to them and hopefully find a way to live a better life.

Life is very powerful, regardless of murderers who believe that there's nothing wrong with killing people.

Many murderers love to live and don't want anyone to take their lives, and many of them won't even think about taking their own life because God created life to be very powerful for good and bad people to want to live every day in this world.

Life is very powerful for everyone in their right mind to have no excuse to not live life unto the Lord Jesus Christ, who is the all-powerful, eternal life that we will miss out on if we live our lives in rebellion against God.

There are people who have taken their own lives because they didn't believe that they had something good to live for.

That doesn't change that life is very powerful to live and most people in this world love to live.

We can't judge people who take their own lives, but it's never a good thing to do this because God gave us His great wealth of life that we can spend up and live in the poverty of sin if we don't live our lives unto Jesus Christ, who is the all-powerful eternal life.

We Can Always be Thankful

We can always be thankful unto the Lord.

The reason why many people worry about things is because they are not thankful unto the Lord.

The reason why many people complain is because they are not thankful unto the Lord.

The reason why many people get depressed is because they are not thankful unto the Lord.

Being thankful unto the Lord will lift us up out of the pits of worry.

Being thankful unto the Lord will lift us up out of the pits of complaining.

Being thankful unto the Lord will lift us up out of the pits of depression.

How can we worry and be thankful unto the Lord at the same time?

How can we complain and be thankful unto the Lord at the same time?

Can we feel depressed and be thankful unto the Lord at the same time?

We can only do one or the other.

Being thankful unto the Lord will give us a very positive outlook on our lives.

We can always be thankful unto the Lord as long as we have life, even if our health is not good.

We can always be thankful unto the Lord as long as we live, even if we don't have much money.

We can always be thankful unto the Lord as long as we live, because life is from the Lord, no matter how bad that life can get for you and me who can put our hope and faith in the Lord, even if He didn't answer our prayers on our time.

We can be thankful that the Lord doesn't always answer our prayers on our time, because that is not always on time.

Being thankful unto the Lord is for life on our good days and bad days.

We can always thank the Lord for giving us a mind to think.

We can always thank the Lord for giving us a heart to feel.

Even if we didn't have eyes to see, couldn't hear and couldn't walk, we could still be thankful unto the Lord, who can use our handicaps to be a blessing to others who should also be thankful unto Him.

We can always be thankful unto the Lord as long as we live, no matter how bad off we are, because that can't override the Lord who can make our lives much better just like He did for Job.

There are no bad effects on our lives for being thankful unto the Lord, no matter how bad we may feel.

If we are feeling bad and going through something bad, being thankful unto the Lord can truly lift us up and cause us to feel much better.

We can always be thankful unto the Lord, no matter what we go through in life, because if we think that we are bad off we need to realize there are people who are much worse off than you and me and they may be truly thankful unto the Lord.

Being thankful unto the Lord can surely help get our minds off of the things that can worry us and depress us.

There is so much to thank the Lord for every day that we can't thank the Lord enough for His love, mercy, truth and grace.

We can't thank the Lord enough for giving us life, even if our health might not be so good.

We can be thankful for just being alive, which the devil hates because he knows that as long as we are alive we can choose to believe in Jesus Christ and be saved.

There are people who are blind and are thankful unto the Lord.

There are people who are deaf and are thankful unto the Lord.

There are people who can't walk and are thankful unto the Lord.

There are people who have no arms and are thankful unto the Lord.

There are people who have no hands and are thankful unto the Lord.

There are people who have no legs and are thankful unto the Lord.

There are people who are very poor and are thankful unto the Lord.

Being thankful unto the Lord can ease our worries.

Being thankful unto the Lord can silence our complaints.

There is power in being thankful unto the Lord, who will power us up with mental, emotional and spiritual strength for being thankful unto Him every day.

No one can judge anyone else because only the Lord knows all of our hearts and what we can bear and can't bear.

We can be thankful unto the Lord for knowing us completely when we don't fully know ourselves and can doubt what Jesus can do for us and wallow in that doubt instead of being thankful unto the Lord.

Prayer Can

The truth will set us free from the devil's lies, but prayer can protect us while we drive on the road.

The truth will set us free from the devil's lies, while we sleep all night long.

The truth will set us free from the devil's lies, but prayer can heal us if we are sick.

The truth will set us free from the devil's lies, but prayer can work out our problems in life.

The truth will set us free from the devil's lies, but prayer can ease our minds from worry.

The truth will set us free from the devil's lies, but prayer can change things.

The truth will set us free from the devil's lies, but prayer can open doors that no one can close.

The truth will set us free from the devil's lies, but prayer can protect us from harm and danger.

The truth will set us free from the devil's lies, but prayer can give us the strength to keep holding on.

The truth will set us free from the devil's lies, but prayer can make the devil tremble.

The truth will set us free from the devil's lies, but prayer can make the devil flee.

The truth will set us free from the devil's lies, but prayer can cause a sinner to confess and repent.

The truth will set us free from the devil's lies, but prayer can cause you and me to surrender all of our hearts to Jesus Christ.

The truth will set us free from the devil's lies, but prayer can take our doubts and fears up to God in heaven.

The truth will set us free from the devil's lies, but prayer can cause God to allow us to live one hundred or more years.

The truth will set us free from the devil's lies, but prayer can surely give us the power and strength to live the truth unto Jesus Christ, who stayed in prayer and lived the truth unto God when Jesus lived on earth without sin.

The devil hates the truth and the devil hates prayer because it is so very powerful and makes the devil tremble.

The devil hates the truth and the devil hates prayer that is very powerful and makes the devil flee from us.

The devil hates the truth and the devil hates prayer because those two things work together to prolong our lives.

The devil hates the truth and the devil hates prayer because those two things will change anyone's life for the better to love Jesus and keep His Commandments.

The devil will always hate the truth of God's holy word that is for you and me to live by to be like Jesus, who stayed in prayer unto God when He lived on earth without sin.

The devil will always hate our prayers unto Jesus because he knows that Jesus will give us the power to overcome his evil schemes if we believe that Jesus can do anything but fail us.

A Day to Rejoice

When someone is getting baptized to die to self and give their life to the Lord, it's a day for all the spiritual brothers and sisters in the church to rejoice.

Seeing someone getting baptized is a wonderful thing to witness to because that spiritual brother or spiritual sister is showing you and me that they want to live for Jesus Christ just like you and I do.

All the angels in heaven will rejoice over one sinner who gives his or her heart to the Lord.

Oh, what a great day to rejoice over someone getting baptized in the church where he or she will go down under the water to die to self in the baptism pool and come back up being a new creature in our Lord and Savior Jesus Christ, who no one can beat rejoicing over souls won to Him.

Oh, what a day to greatly rejoice and celebrate over a born-again believer in Jesus Christ.

The strait and narrow road is not easy to walk on but it takes us to Jesus non-stop so that we can rejoice about every day.

All who have been baptized in the Holy Spirit are new creatures in Jesus Christ.

Being baptized in the Holy Spirit is true conviction and conversion to go down under the water and come back up out of the water being all about living for Jesus.

Anybody can go down under the water in the baptism pool, but only a real, true believer in Jesus Christ will come back up out of the water being a changed man, woman, boy or girl who wants to love Jesus and keep His Commandments.

Many people will say that you can be a dry devil before going down under the water in the baptism pool, and a wet devil coming back up out of the water in the baptism pool.

That is for people who are not baptized in the Holy Spirit being a spiritual baptism with a whole-heart of surrender unto the Lord.

The physical baptism can only be an outward show with pretense without the spiritual baptism of the Holy Spirit who causes God to rejoice and be happy to put a new creature to work for Him spreading the gospel of Jesus Christ.

One Church Body

We all are from different walks of life, but we all are one church body in Jesus Christ.

We all come together from different walks of life to unite in one church body.

There are people who preach in the church.

There are people who teach in the church.

There are people who sing in the church.

There are people who are authors in the church.

There are people who give encouragement in the church.

There are people who give hospitality in the church.

There are people who do plays in the church.

There are people who give a health message in the church.

There are people who give a lot of money to the church.

There are people who do community service work in the church.

There are people who usher in the church.

There are people who pray in the church.

There are people who organize things in the church.

There are people who administrate things in the church.

There are people who talk a lot in the church.

There are people who are quiet in the church.

There are people who heal in the church.

There are people who give a helping hand in the church.

There are people who are very intelligent in the church.

There are people who have common sense in the church.

We all are one church body with different body parts working together to build up the church of Jesus Christ.

We all are one body with different body parts working together to spread the gospel of Jesus Christ.

There are people who play music in the church.

There are people who have good judgment in the church.

There are people who are educated in the church.

There are people who are wise in the church.

We all are from different walks of life and come together as one church body in Jesus Christ.

We all come together to worship Jesus and love and obey Jesus and give Jesus all the glory and praise because Jesus is the head of the church body and blesses each body part so it works sufficiently to win souls to him.

God Commands Us to Love Our Neighbors

God commands us to love our neighbors who are everybody in our family.

God commands love our neighbors who are everybody in our neighborhood.

God commands us to love our neighbors who are everybody on our jobs.

God commands us to love our neighbors who are everybody driving on the highways and local roads.

God commands us to love our neighbors who are everybody in the stores.

God commands us to love our neighbors who are everybody in our state.

God commands us to love our neighbors who are everybody in our country.

God commands us to love our neighbors who are everybody in this world.

Criminals don't love their neighbors who they will kill.

Criminals don't love their neighbors who they will rob.

Criminals don't love their neighbors who they will maim.

Criminals don't love their neighbors who they will abuse.

Criminals don't love their neighbors who they will rape.

Criminals don't love their neighbors who they will tell lies on.

Criminals don't love their neighbors who they will use.

Criminals don't love their neighbors who they will cheat.

God commands us to love our neighbors, even though our neighbors can be hard to love.

It's hard to love people who will lie on us.

It's hard to love people who will use us.

It's hard to love people who will cheat us.

It's hard to love people who will rob us.

It's hard to love people who will kill us.

It's hard to love people who will maim us.

It's hard to love people who will abuse us.

It's hard to love people who will hate us.

It's hard to love people who will disrespect us.

It's hard to love people who will judge us.

It's hard to love people who will want what belongs to us.

It's hard to love people who are our enemies.

God commands us to love our neighbors who are everybody, whether they are good or bad.

God commands us to love our neighbors who are everybody, whether they are rich or poor.

God commands us to love our neighbors who are everybody, whether they are a criminal or a Christian.

If we don't love everybody and say that we love God, then we are lying because God loves everybody.

If we love God, we will love our neighbors who are everybody in this world.

You and I can say that we are Christians, but if we don't love everybody inside the church and outside the church we are liars.

We can go to church all of our lives and hold office positions, but if we don't love our neighbors who are everybody, we are not saved in Jesus Christ who loves everybody and gave up His life on the cross to save everybody from their sins.

The Bible says that the greatest gift is love, and even many church folks will only love those who can benefit them in their ministry work in the church.

We all want to go to heaven, but first we must love our neighbors who are everybody who God loves.

If we don't love our neighbors, then how can we love God?

God and our neighbors go hand in hand here on Earth, and it will be the same way up in heaven where there is nothing but everlasting love.

God commands us to love our neighbors who are everybody on earth.

God commands us to love everybody the same because there won't be any partial love up in heaven where we want to go.

There won't be any loveless people going to heaven; they will only live on earth.

God commands us to love our neighbors who are everybody in this world

Everybody, even in the church, won't love you and me, but they can't stop you and me from loving them if we love Jesus Christ.

Partial love is loving some people more than other people, but it won't be that way in heaven.

Partially loving people will only love certain people like those in their circle of friends who they would love to see in heaven, but there won't be any partial love in heaven.

God commands us to love our neighbors who are everybody in our family, the church and in the world.

When Jesus lived in this world without sin, Jesus loved everybody the same way with no partial love, because He gave up His life on the cross to save everybody, even His enemies, from being lost in their sins.

There will only be one hundred percent eternal love for everybody who will make it to heaven when Jesus Christ comes back again.

No partial loving people and no Loveless people will be our neighbors in heaven where God's eternal, wholesome love was demonstrated through His only begotten Son, Jesus Christ, who was rejected by partial loving people who couldn't make up their minds to follow Him.

Jesus was rejected by Loveless people who tried to kill Him before He was nailed on the cross for the sins of all the world.

God commands us to love our neighbors who are everybody breathing with life in their bodies.

There is only one way to truly love, that is to love all of our neighbors who are everybody who God loves but hate everybody's sins.

God commands us to love our neighbors who are everybody in this world.

If we don't love even one person, we don't love God who leaves nobody out of His love, mercy and grace.

We should love everybody, but we shouldn't love anybody more than we love God whose love will never fail to not love everybody the same when our love can fail to not love everybody the same, especially our enemies.

God foreknew that it wouldn't be easy for you and me to love partial loving people and loveless people who God loves but hates their sins.

God commands us to love our neighbors who are everybody, even partial loving people and loveless people, whether they go to church or don't go to church.

God commands us to love our neighbors who are everybody in this world where God will separate the wheat from the tares.

God will sooner or later separate the partial loving people and the loveless people from His wholesome, loving children who will go with His Son, Jesus Christ, back to heaven when Jesus comes back again.

If We Can

If we can breathe air in and out of our nostrils, we can believe in Jesus Christ who created the air for us to breathe in and out of our nostrils.

If we can dream away in the night where our dreams can change from one scene to the next scene, we can believe in Jesus Christ who can make us dreams to come true.

Joseph had dreams from God, who made his dreams come true and caused Joseph to become the governor of Egypt.

If we can choose to think on and talk about magic and spells, we can choose to believe in Jesus Christ who the bible tells us about casting out demons from people and gave power to his disciples to cast out demons too.

If we can talk to people we don't know, we can believe in Jesus Christ and get to know Him who will always be on time to answer our prayers so we will know that He is for us.

If we can talk our own words into actions to be seen, we can believe in Jesus Christ who is the Word of God who was made flesh and lived without sin in all of His words and actions.

If we have strength in our bodies to move around here and there, we can believe in Jesus Christ who will give us His holy spirit to move us in doing good deeds to spread the good news about Him coming back again to take us to heaven if we are saved in our Lord and Savior Jesus Christ, who everybody will not believe in.

There are People Who Believe

There are people who believe that Moses was a magician because he parted the Red Sea.

There are people who believe that Jesus Christ was only a prophet, not the Son of God.

There are people who believe that religion is only an idea made up by weak-minded people.

There are people who believe that the bible is an imaginary book written by delusional men who wanted to draw attention to themselves.

There are people who believe that there is no God – they see Him as make-believe for especially poor people.

There are people who believe that there is no devil, and that he was made up by stupid people who have no intelligence.

There are people who believe that they are gods and have all the power because of their riches and wealth.

There are people who believe that they are perfect and have no sins, even though they sin against God by just believing that lie.

There are people who believe that a miracle is luck that can be bad, but there is nothing bad about a miracle from God who will never change and will stay the same way forever and ever.

Luck is unstable and can change and has no foundation to let it stand day after day.

If we believe in Jesus Christ, the devil and his demons will tremble because they know that Jesus is real and that He has all the power over false beliefs.

This is why Lucifer did not succeed in his battle in heaven, because Jesus had the power to cast out the devil and his fallen angels.

It's Very Rare These Days

It's very rare these days for people to have outdoor toilets like those still used today in some other countries.

It's very rare these days that people have washboards to wash their clothes with.

It's very rare these days that people have screened-in porches.

It's very rare these days that people have rotary dial phones.

It's very rare these days that people have record players.

It's very rare these days that people have eight track tapes.

It's very rare these days that people have jukeboxes.

It's very rare these days that people have two-dollar bills.

It's very rare these days that people have black and white TV screens.

It's very rare these days that people have a wooden house.

It's very rare these days that people have milk trucks delivering milk.

It's very rare these days that people see an ice cream truck.

It's very rare these days that people have a lucky charm.

It's very rare these days that people have a silver dollar.

It's very rare these days that people have a stove that burns wood and coal.

It's very rare these days that people have patience.

It's very rare these days that people have humility.

It's very rare these days that people have common sense.

It's very rare these days that people who go to church have the Holy Spirit.

It's very rare these days that many people who go to church have Jesus Christ in their hearts.

It Can Cause Our Hearts to Hurt

For all of us animal lovers, if we have animals that we kept since they were young it can cause our hearts to hurt when our animals get old.

They can get old and slow down instead of running very fast, which can cause our hearts to hurt.

If we can have a heart for animals not being created in God's image, then we can have a heart for human beings who God created in His image.

We know that animals can love us if we love them, but we can't be sure about human beings who we can love but might not love us in return.

If we can be lovers of animals that don't look like us, then we can be lovers of human beings who God sent his Son into this world to save from their sins.

God didn't send His Son into this world to save animals that didn't sin against him.

Sin came into this world through a human being, not through an animal that can't choose right from wrong.

Many people will love their pets more than they love human beings who can do a lot more for them than their pets.

It's good to love the animals that God loves every day.

Most of all, God commands us to love human beings every day, regardless of many human beings acting like untamed animals and making the tame animals seem to have more civilized ways than them.

It can cause our hearts to hurt when we see and hear about human beings killing human beings because they look different.

Many human beings who have no heart are those same human beings who love to kill other human beings no matter if they are adults or children.

If our hearts hurt, it is because we have love for human beings and animals that God created for His pleasure.

Jesus was the Greatest War Veteran

Jesus was the greatest war veteran who fought against Lucifer and his angels and cast them out of heaven.

Jesus was the first five-star general over all of His angels in heaven who fought the greatest war that Lucifer and his angels were doomed to lose.

Jesus was the greatest war veteran who laid down His weapons and humbled Himself here on earth where He could have caused all the Pharisees, religious leaders and Roman soldiers to drop dead with just one spoken word.

Jesus was the greatest war veteran who survived in the wilderness for forty days and forty nights of prayer and fasting to defeat the devil's temptations.

Jesus was the greatest war veteran who survived in the wilderness for forty days and forty nights while He fought against the devil's temptations with the word of God that is sharper than a two-edged sword.

Jesus was the greatest veteran to win the war in heaven and He was the greatest war veteran who fought against all of the devil's temptations with a successful plan to lay down His life on the cross to save you and me from our sins.

The devil believed that he had defeated Jesus who became sin on the cross and died a terrible death that the devil conquered over Jesus for only two days.

Jesus rose from the grave to win the greatest war on earth, surely being the spiritual war that no man can fight in and win against the devil and his angels without Jesus being his top commanding five-star general of the heavens.

Jesus is the greatest war veteran who will one day rain down fire and brimstone on the devil and his angels and his human agents after Jesus raises the wicked dead in the second resurrection here on earth.

Jesus will win that war against the devil and his fallen angels and his human agents who will surround the new Jerusalem holy city to attack it with no success and be defeated by Jesus and sentenced to burn in hell.

Addicted to Pulling the Trigger

Many people are addicted to pulling the trigger on a gun and shooting down people who they hate.

People are addicted to pulling the trigger on a loaded gun and shooting down people who they want to get revenge on.

Many people are addicted to pulling the trigger on a gun and shooting down people because they look different from them.

Even some little children are addicted to pulling the trigger on a loaded gun because they just don't know any better.

Many people are addicted to pulling the trigger on the loaded gun of their words and shooting down people with bullets of jealousy.

Many people are addicted to pulling the trigger on the loaded gun of their words and shooting down people with bullets of gossip.

Many people are addicted to pulling the trigger on the loaded gun of their words and shooting down people with bullets of strife.

Many people are addicted to pulling the trigger on the loaded gun of their words to shoot people down with the bullets of their anger.

Many people are addicted to pulling the trigger on the loaded gun of their actions to shoot people down with the bullets of their violence.

Many people are addicted to pulling the trigger on the loaded gun of their actions to shoot down people with the bullets of their abuse.

Back in the Bible days, Pharisees and religious leaders were addicted to pulling the trigger on the loaded gun of their words to shoot down Jesus with the bullets of their jealousy.

Back in the Bible days, there were no real guns that the Pharisees and religious leaders could have used to shoot down Jesus, but if there had been real guns back in the Bible days they would have done it.

Many people today are addicted to pulling the trigger on a loaded gun to shoot people down without thinking twice about it because they are so trigger happy to kill people no matter what age they are.

Jesus Christ, our Lord, has jammed up the spiritual loaded gun of the devil so it can't shoot us down with his temptations that would kill us spiritually if Jesus had not shed His blood on the cross and died to save us from our sins when He rose from the grave with the victory over death.

You and I can spiritually shoot down the devil's lies by living our lives unto Jesus Christ every day.

We can spiritually shoot down the devil's lies by loving and obeying Jesus Christ.

Many Christians are addicted to pulling the trigger on the loaded gun of their actions, especially to shoot down ignorant people with the bullets of their wrongdoings when they know to do what is right by God's holy word.

Use Your

Use your genius for Jesus and not for the devil.

Use your brilliance for Jesus and not for the devil.

Use your intelligence for Jesus and not for the devil.

Use your education for Jesus and not for the devil.

Use your mind for Jesus and not for the devil.

Use your heart for Jesus and not for the devil.

Use your wealth for Jesus and not for the devil.

Use your body for Jesus and not for the devil.

Use your motives for Jesus and not for the devil.

Use your intentions for Jesus and not for the devil.

Use your freedom for Jesus and not for the devil.

Use your time for Jesus and not for the devil.

Use your talents for Jesus and not for the devil.

Use your skills for Jesus and not for the devil.

Your house for Jesus and not for the devil.

Use your vehicles for Jesus and not for the devil.

Use your apartment for Jesus and not for the devil.

Use your boat for Jesus and not for the devil.

Use your airplane for Jesus and not for the devil.

Use your business for Jesus and not for the devil.

Use your wardrobe for Jesus and not for the devil.

Use your mouth for Jesus and not for the devil.

Use your eyes for Jesus and not for the devil.

Use your hands Jesus and not for the devil.

Use your feet for Jesus and not for the devil.

Use your life for Jesus and not for the devil.

If you and I use everything that we have for Jesus Christ, we can't go wrong in this world where we will do ourselves wrong if we use even one thing that we have for the devil.

Our Minds can Drift Off In

Our minds can drift off into the uncertain if we don't keep our minds on Jesus.

Our minds can drift off in judging people, if we don't keep our minds on Jesus.

Our minds can drift off in holding a grudge, if we don't keep our minds on Jesus.

Our minds can drift off in anger, if keep our minds on Jesus.

Our minds can drift off in negativity, if we don't keep our minds on Jesus.

Our minds can drift off in envy, if we don't keep our minds on Jesus.

Our minds can drift off in covetousness, if we don't keep our minds on Jesus.

Our minds can drift off in greed, if we don't keep our minds on Jesus.

Our minds can drift off in lust, if we don't keep her minds on Jesus.

Our minds can drift off in fear, if we don't keep our minds on Jesus.

Our minds can drift off in favoritism, if we don't keep our minds on Jesus.

Our minds can drift off in insecurity, if we don't keep our minds on Jesus.

Our minds can drift off in pride, if we don't keep our minds on Jesus.

Our minds can drift off in worry, if we don't keep our minds on Jesus.

Our minds can drift off in depression, if we don't keep our minds on Jesus.

Our minds can drift off in discontentment, if we don't keep our minds on Jesus.

Our minds can drift off in confusion, if we don't keep our minds on Jesus.

Our minds can drift off in discouragement, if we don't keep our minds on Jesus.

Our minds can drift off in schemes, if we don't keep our minds on Jesus.

Our minds can drift off in unrealistic thoughts, if we don't keep our minds on Jesus.

Our minds can drift off in the imaginary, if we don't keep our minds on Jesus.

Our minds can drift off in self, if we don't keep our minds on Jesus.

Our minds can drift off in ignorance, if we don't keep our minds on Jesus.

Our minds can drift off in foolishness, if we don't keep our minds on Jesus.

Our minds can drift off in evilness, if we don't keep our minds on Jesus.

Our minds can drift off in sin, if we don't keep our minds on Jesus.

We must keep our minds stayed on Jesus Christ, who is the only one who can renew our minds to think on pure, righteous thoughts every day.

Our minds can drift off in revenge, if we don't keep our minds on Jesus.

Our minds can drift off in delusion, if we don't keep our minds on Jesus.

Our minds can drift off in spiritualism, if we don't keep our minds on Jesus.

Our minds can drift off in rebellion, if we don't keep our minds on Jesus.

We keep our minds on Jesus by staying in prayer unto Jesus.

We keep our minds on Jesus by reading the Holy Bible.

We keep our minds on Jesus by choosing to live our lives unto Jesus Christ every day.

We keep our minds on Jesus by having faith in Him, even through our trials, and knowing that Jesus will use these to strengthen our minds to always think on Him.

Doesn't Mean Anything Good at All

Paying the mortgage doesn't mean anything good at all, if we don't return a faithful tithe and offering unto the Lord.

Paying the rent doesn't mean anything good at all, if we don't return a faithful tithe and offering unto the Lord.

Paying the utility bill doesn't mean anything good at all, if we don't return a faithful tithe and offering unto the Lord.

Paying the car bill doesn't mean anything good at all, if we don't return a faithful tithe and offering unto the Lord.

Paying our bills doesn't mean anything good at all, if we don't return a faithful tithe and offering unto the Lord.

Getting a federal and state tax return doesn't mean anything good at all if we don't return a faithful tithe and offering unto the Lord.

Buying some new clothes doesn't mean anything good at all, if we don't return a faithful tithe and offering unto the Lord.

Buying some new shoes doesn't mean anything good at all, if we don't return faithful tithes and offerings unto the Lord.

Buying a new house doesn't mean anything good at all, if we don't return faithful tithes and offerings unto the Lord.

Buying a new car and new truck doesn't mean anything at all, if we don't return faithful tithes and offerings unto the Lord.

Buying a new computer and a new phone doesn't mean anything good at all, if we don't return faithful tithes and offerings unto the Lord.

Being rich doesn't mean anything good at all, if we don't return faithful tithes and offerings unto the Lord.

Just having an income doesn't mean anything good at all, if we don't return faithful tithes and offerings unto the Lord.

The tithes and offerings belong to the Lord, who truly owns all of our money and everything that we have.

All the Lord asks for is only one-tenth of our earnings as tithes and free will offerings.

The Lord could have asked for nine-tenths of our income, but the Lord knows that we need the nine-tenths to live off of day by day.

The Lord is not greedy and will not ask us for more than one-tenth as our tithes and free will offerings.

Many people are greedy and hold onto the one-tenth and don't tithe or make a free will offering to the Lord.

So, let's not be greedy and hold back our tithes and offerings unto the Lord, who promised us that He will open the windows of heaven and pour out His blessings until they overflow upon us.

Whether we are rich, upper middle class, middle class, lower middle or poor, we must return faithful tithes and free will offerings unto the Lord because it truly helps us to not be selfish and greedy, when the Lord is always so giving to us with His love, mercy, and salvation that we don't deserve to receive from Him day after day.

Live For

Many people live for wealth.

A few people live for content.

Many people live for sex.

A few people live for celibacy.

Many people live for ignorance.

A few people live for knowledge.

Many people live for divorce.

A few people live for marriage.

Many people live for material things.

A few people live for spiritual things.

Many people live for favoritism.

A few people live for respect to all.

Many people live for rejection.

A few people live for acceptance.

Many people live for superiority.

A few people live for equality.

Many people live for hate.

A few people live for love.

A few people live for work.

Many people live for laziness.

A few people live for peace.

Many people live for strife.

A few people live for truth.

Many people live for lies.

Many people live for pride.

A few people live for humility.

Many people live for bad news.

A few people live for good news.

Many people live for the present.

A few people live for the future.

A few people live for good.

Many people live for evil.

A few people live for the head of the church.

Many people live for the church.

A few people live for God, the Father, the Son and the Holy Spirit.

Many people live for the devil.

A few people live for the law.

Many people live for lawlessness.

A few people live for fairness.

Many people live for injustice.

Many people live for religion.

A few people live for Jesus Christ.

Many people live for foolishness.

A few people live for keeping God's Ten Commandments.

Many people live for hell.

A few people live for heaven.

Goes Down the Drain Like Water

Success in this life goes down the drain like water but when it comes to eternal life, success is eternal in Jesus Christ.

Achievement in this life goes down the drain like water but when it comes to eternal life, achievement is eternal in Jesus Christ.

Riches in this life go down the drain like water but when it comes to eternal life, riches are eternal in Jesus Christ.

Greatness in this life goes down the drain like water but when it comes to eternal life, greatness is eternal in Jesus Christ.

Good health in this life goes down the drain like water but when it comes to eternal life, good health is eternal in Jesus Christ.

Genius in this life goes down the drain like water but when it comes to eternal life, genius is eternal in Jesus Christ.

Technology in this life goes down the drain like water but when it comes to eternal life, technology is eternal in Jesus Christ.

Education in this life goes down the drain like water but when it comes to eternal life, education is eternal in Jesus Christ.

Talent in this life goes down the drain like water but when it comes to eternal life, talent is eternal in Jesus Christ.

Skill in this life goes down the drain like water but when it comes to eternal life, skill is eternal in Jesus Christ.

Beauty in this life goes down the drain like water but when it comes to eternal life, beauty is eternal in Jesus Christ.

Work in this life goes down the drain like water but when it comes to eternal life, work is eternal in Jesus Christ.

Youth in this life goes down the drain like water but when it comes to eternal life, youth is eternal in Jesus Christ.

Everything in this world goes down the drain like water but when it comes to eternal life, there will one day be an eternal new world in Jesus Christ.

It's Always Good

It's always good to talk a lot about Jesus and not a lot about people who can depress you.

It's always good to talk a lot about Jesus and not a lot about people who can disappoint you.

It's always good to talk a lot about Jesus and not a lot about people who can discourage you.

It's always good to talk a lot about Jesus and not a lot about people who can let you down.

It's always good to talk a lot about Jesus and not a lot about people who couldn't care less about you.

It's always good to talk a lot about Jesus and not a lot about people who can change on you.

It's always good to talk a lot about Jesus and not a lot about people who can worry you.

It's always good to talk a lot about Jesus and not a lot about people who can hurt you.

It's always good to talk a lot about Jesus and not a lot about people who can deceive you.

It's always good to talk a lot about Jesus and not a lot about people who can lie to you.

It's always good to talk a lot about Jesus and not a lot about people who can lie on you.

It's always good to talk a lot about Jesus and not a lot about people who can make you sick.

It's always good to talk a lot about Jesus and not a lot about people who can turn their back on you.

It's always good to talk a lot about Jesus and not a lot about people who can talk bad about you.

It's always good to talk a lot about Jesus and not a lot about people who can use you.

It's always good to talk a lot about Jesus and not a lot about people who can gossip about you.

It's always good to talk a lot about Jesus and not a lot about people who can hate you.

It's always good to talk a lot about Jesus and not a lot about people who can pretend with you.

It's always good to talk a lot about Jesus and not a lot about people who can put you down.

It's always good to talk a lot about Jesus and not a lot about people who can get jealous of you.

It's always good to talk a lot about Jesus and not a lot about people who can rob you.

It's always good to talk a lot about Jesus and not a lot about people who can kill you.

It's always good to talk a lot about Jesus who has no sins.

It's always good to talk a lot about Jesus and not a lot about people who have sins to confess and repent of unto Jesus Christ who is the only One who can save us from our sins.

The Only Book

The bible is the only book that we can read to know all the truth about sinful men.

The bible is the only book that we can read to know all the truth about the devil.

The bible is the only book that we can read to know all the truth about God.

The bible is the only book that we can read to know all the truth about Jesus Christ

The bible is the only book that we can read to know all the truth about evil.

The bible is the only book that we can read to know all the truth about love.

The bible is the only book that we can read to know all the truth about the past.

The bible is the only book that we can read to know all the truth about the present.

The bible is the only book that we can read to know all the truth about the future.

The bible is the only book that we can read to know all the truth about people.

The bible is the only book that we can read to know all the truth about ourselves.

The bible is the only book that we can read to know all the truth about this world.

The bible is the only book that we can read to know all the truth about life.

The bible is the only book that we can read to know all the truth about health.

The bible is the only book that we can read to know all the truth about suffering.

The bible is the only book that we can read to know all the truth about living right.

The bible is the only book that we can read to know all the truth about death.

The bible is the only book that we can read to know all the truth about life after death.

The bible is the only book that we can read to know all the truth about heaven.

The bible is the only book that we can read to know all the truth about existence.

The bible is the only book that we can read to know all the truth beyond our opinions.

The bible is the only book that we can read to know all the truth that will set us free from the devil's lies.

The bible is the only book that we can read to know all the truth about Jesus Christ being the savior of the world.

The bible is the only book that we can read to know all the truth about Jesus saving us from our sins.

The bible is the only book that we can read to know all the truth about Jesus Christ coming back again to take you and me and all of His children to heaven.

The bible is the only book that we can read to know all the truth about our destiny.

God Surely Knew What He was Doing

God surely knew what He was doing when He created a woman for a man.

When God created Eve for Adam, all of God's other creations must have marveled at Eve's presence in the Garden of Eden.

When God created the opposite sex for Adam, all of the angels in heaven must have rejoiced.

Good Christian women, especially, are a blessing to talk to.

God surely knew what He was doing when he put Adam to sleep and molded and shaped a woman from Adam's rib.

When Adam woke up, he must have been very well pleased to see his soulmate being so close beside him.

Adam must have felt like he was on top of the world when he saw Eve looking more beautiful than all the other creatures God had created.

God created a woman for a man, and the devil will never succeed in destroying the marriage between a man and a woman.

Many men are marrying men and many women are marrying women, but it will never cause a marriage between a man and a woman to be out of date.

God surely knew what He was doing when He created a woman for a man.

God didn't create a man for a man or a woman for a woman.

God is perfect to make no mistakes because it's the devil who makes the mistakes of trying to make God's creations look so deformed, especially through evolution.

God surely knew what he was doing when He created a woman for a man.

Most men love to be with a woman and most women love to be with a man.

It comes to show that God was right to create a woman for a man.

Many men and many women who love to be with the same sex are surely not what God created to be that way.

God surely knew what He was doing when He created a woman for a man.

Even a male animal will not have an attraction for another male animal.

A female animal will not have an attraction for another female animal.

God didn't create the animals in his image, and the animals know not to do anything unnatural, but many men and woman will do that.

God is against this because God created a woman to be with a man.

Why would God want a man to have an attraction for another man?

Why would God want a woman to have an attraction for another woman?

What kind of God would want that when the bible says God created a woman for a man.

God created Eve for Adam.

God wanted a man to be attracted to a woman and God wanted a woman to be attracted to a man.

God would not have created a woman for a man if He wanted a man to be with a man.

If God had created a man for a man, there would be no population of people in this world today.

A man cannot procreate with another man and a woman cannot procreate with another woman.

God surely knew what He was doing when He created a woman for a man to procreate the billions of human beings who live in this world today.

If the Lord Questions Us

If the Lord questions us, how will we answer Him?

If the Lord questions us about what we think, how will we answer Him who knows what we will think before we think it?

If the Lord questions us about what we say, how will we answer Him who knows what we will say before we say it?

If the Lord questions us about what we do, how will we answer Him who knows what we will do before we do it?

If the Lord questions us about what we feel in our hearts, how will we answer Him who knows what we will feel before we feel anything in our hearts?

If the Lord questions us about our lives, how will we answer Him who knows all about our lives including things we don't know about?

When we sleep in the night, we don't know if we will wake up again to live our lives doing our own will or doing the Lord's will.

If the Lord questions us, will we be strong enough to handle His question and answer it?

If the Lord questions us, will we be wise enough to answer His question?

If the Lord questions us, will we be knowledgeable enough to answer His question?

If the Lord questions us, will we be experienced enough to answer His question?

If the Lord questions us, will we be faithful enough to answer His question?

If the Lord questions us, will we be obedient enough to answer His question?

If the Lord questions us, will we be holy enough to answer His question?

If the Lord questions us, will we be prepared enough to answer His question?

People can question us and we may not answer their question because we might not know how to answer it.

If we can't answer every question that people ask us, then how can we answer just one question from the Lord, whose question is too profound for us to answer it?

If we are not filled with the holy spirit, who interprets to God what we really mean to say from our hearts, how will we give our answer to the Lord's question?

In This World Today

In this world today, you can think you are looking at a woman, but it may be a man.

In this world today, you can think you are looking at a man, but it may be a woman.

In this world today, you can think you are giving some money to a woman or man holding up a sign asking for help, but they may be living in a big beautiful house.

In this world today, you can think an educated man or woman has themselves together, but he or she might be making foolish choices in their lives.

In this world today, you can think that a man dressed up in a suit can do you no wrong, but a criminal can wear a suit and look so innocent every day.

In this world today, you can think you truly know your child, but he or she might be keeping secrets from you and you won't know that they're struggling with some inappropriate behaviors.

In this world today, you can think you truly know your spouse, but they may be keeping secrets from you.

You just don't know who you are married to until someone else tells you the truth about your spouse and then you have to either believe it or not believe it.

In this world today, you and I can think we are so strong in the Lord and do whatever He tells us to do.

The Lord will surely test us for us to know if we will truly represent Him before others who may test us to see if we are true Christians who live what we talk or even write about Jesus Christ.

O Lord, Help Me

O Lord, help me to not lie to anyone.

O Lord, help me to not lie on anyone.

O Lord, help me to not steal from anyone.

O Lord, help me to not kill anyone.

O Lord, help me to not to cheat anyone.

O Lord, help me to not hurt anyone.

O Lord, help me to not abuse anyone.

O Lord, help me to not use anyone.

O Lord, help me to not to be jealous of anyone.

O Lord, help me to not to envy anyone.

O Lord, help me to not want what belongs to someone else.

O Lord, help me to not put anyone down.

O Lord, help me to not talk bad about anyone.

O Lord, help me to not treat anyone bad.

O Lord, help me to not hate anyone.

O Lord, help me to not disrespect anyone.

O Lord, help me to not be rude to anyone.

O Lord, help me to not give anyone a bad name.

O Lord, help me to not ruin anyone's name.

O Lord, help me to not discourage anyone.

O Lord, help me to not disappoint anyone.

O Lord, help me to not judge anyone.

O Lord, help me to not deceive anyone.

O Lord, help me to not give anyone an evil eye look.

O Lord, help me to not get revenge back at anyone.

O Lord, help me to not hold grudges against anyone.

O Lord, help me to not trick anyone.

O Lord, help me to not try to control anyone.

O Lord, help me to not care less about anyone.

O Lord, help me to not be mean to anyone.

O Lord, help me to not make trouble for anyone.

O Lord, help me to not quarrel with anyone.

O Lord, help me to not fight with anyone.

O Lord, help me to not treat anyone unfairly.

O Lord, help me to not neglect anyone.

O Lord, help me to not show favoritism to anyone.

O Lord, help me to not cause anyone to stumble into sin.

O Lord, help me to not cause anyone to leave the church.

O Lord, help me to not cause anyone to be lost in their sins.

O Lord, you command me to love my neighbor, as I love myself.

Everybody in the church is my neighbor and everybody in this world is my neighbor, who you, O Lord, command me to love.

O Lord, help me to not be impolite to anyone.

O Lord, help me to not believe that I am better than anyone else.

O Lord, help me to not cause anyone to get ill.

O Lord, help me to love you and love my neighbors for me to love myself.

Can Be Used For

Technology can be used for good and technology can be used for evil.

Science can be used for good and science can be used for evil.

Money can be used for good and money can be used for evil.

Religion can be used for good and religion can be used for evil.

Medicine can be used for good and medicine can be used for evil.

The TV can be used for good and the TV can be used for evil.

Food can be used for good and food can be used for evil.

Computers can be used for good and computers can be used for evil.

Phones can be used for good and phones can be used for evil.

Friendship can be used for good and friendship can be used for evil.

Business can be used for good and business can be used for evil.

A marriage can be used for good and a marriage can be used for evil.

A nation can be used for good and a nation can be used for evil.

The news can be used for good and the news can be used for evil.

A church can be used for good and a church can be used for evil.

The highways and local roads can be used for good and the highways and local roads can be used for evil.

The police force can be used for good and the police force can be used for evil.

Entertainment can be used for good and entertainment can be used for evil.

A neighborhood can be used for good and a neighborhood can be used for evil.

A city can be used for good and a city can be used for evil.

A published book can be used for good and a published book can be used for evil.

A smile can be used for good and a smile can be used for evil.

Words can be used for good and words can be used for evil.

Actions can be used for good and actions can be used for evil.

The mind can be used for good and the mind can be used for evil.

The heart can be used for good and the heart can be used for evil.

The body can be used for good and the body can be used for evil.

God uses the mind, heart and body for good, but the devil uses the mind, heart and body for evil.

God is good all the time and uses everything for good.

The devil is evil all the time and uses everything for evil.

God is good all the time and will always be victorious over evil every day.

Evil cannot get the victory over good that is God all the time.

This world still exists today because God is good to all the world, regardless of all the evilness that is going on in our world.

Genius can be used for good and genius can be used for evil.

Intelligence can be used for good and intelligence can be used for evil.

Education can be used for good and education can be used for evil.

Knowledge can be used for good and knowledge can be used for evil.

Our free will choices can be used for good and our free will choices can be used for evil.

We Have No Time to Waste

We have no time to waste in winning souls to the Lord.

We have no time to waste and sit back and do nothing for the Lord, who will waste no time to save us from our sins.

We have no time to waste away our spiritual gifts that the Lord has given to us to edify the church.

We have no time to waste in spreading the gospel of Jesus Christ.

We have no time to waste in this world where we need to study God's holy word to know that the devil is wasting no time to cause as many souls as he can to be lost.

The devil is wasting no time to fill up hell where he will surely go.

We have no time to waste in the church where we must love our spiritual brothers and sisters like it's our last day to live.

We have no time to waste like there is no tomorrow to get ourselves right with the Lord.

Jesus didn't waste any time coming to this world where he grew up so He could relate to the human race.

Jesus didn't waste any time beginning His ministry after He came out of the wilderness where he was tempted by the devil for forty days and nights.

Jesus didn't waste any time healing the sick, feeding the hungry, opening the eyes of the blind, casting out demons and raising the dead, which he always did on time.

Jesus doesn't waste any time answering our prayers and working things out for us.

If Jesus doesn't answer all of our prayers, he won't waste any time letting us know.

We have no time to waste putting off the opportunity that Jesus gives to us to be a witness of Him with our time, talent and tithes.

We have no time to waste with our life that Jesus gives to us to live doing His holy will in this world.

Many church folks will waste their time doing nothing worthwhile for the Lord, and would rather complain and worry about what they have no control over, when the Lord can remove it like it never existed.

A Day Will Go On About Its Business

A day will go on about its business to bring in the sunshine.

A day will go on about its business to bring in the rain.

A day will go on about its business to bring in the heat.

A day will go on about its business to bring in the cold.

A day will go on about its business to bring in the chill.

A day will go on about its business to bring in a tornado.

A day will go on about its business to bring in a hurricane.

A day will go on about its business to bring in the snow.

A day will go on about its business to bring in the hail.

A day will go on about its business to bring in the fog.

A day will go on about its business to bring in the dew.

A day will go on about its business to bring in the heavy traffic.

A day will go on about its business to bring in good news.

A day will go on about its business to bring in bad news.

A day will go on about its business to bring in a victory.

A day will go on about its business to bring in a defeat.

A day will go on about its business to bring in a cure.

A day will go on about its business to bring in a sickness.

A day will go on about its business to bring in the truth.

A day will go on about its business to bring in lies.

A day will go on about its business to bring in pride.

A day will go on about its business to bring in greed.

A day will go on about its business to bring in lust.

A day will go on about its business to bring in murders.

A day will go on about its business to bring in violence.

A day will go on about its business to bring in deceptions.

A day will go on about its business to bring in luck.

A day will go on about its business to bring in adulterers.

A day will go on about its business to bring in fornication.

A day will go on about its business to bring in poverty.

A day will go on about its business to bring in wealth.

A day will go on about its business to bring in encouragement.

A day will go on about its business to bring in disappointments.

A day will go on about its business to bring in hate.

A day will go on about its business to bring in God's love.

A day will go on about its business to bring in the gospel of Jesus Christ.

A day will go on about its business to bring in salvation to all men, women, boys and girls.

A day will go on about its business to bring in injustice.

A day will go on about its business to bring in justice.

A day will go on about its business to bring in good health.

A day will go on about its business to bring in wickedness.

A day will go on about its business to bring in God's goodness that leads to repentance.

If We had to Work Our Way

If we had to work our way into heaven, then our work would never be good enough for the Lord.

Our works unto the Lord fall short of the glory of God every day.

Our works are so flawed when it comes to Jesus Christ, who lived in this sinful world without sin for his works to be perfect in the presence of God.

Only Jesus can save us from our sins, which is something our works cannot do.

If we had to work our way into heaven, then our works would never please God, who is pleased by our faith in Him.

If we had to work our way into heaven, then our works would be so worthless to God, who loves a pure heart of faith in Him because works without faith are dead to God.

We can't enter into heaven by our works alone because if we don't believe in Jesus Christ, our works are meaningless to God.

Our works are no real proof that we love the Lord, because a wolf in sheep's clothing can work in the church but not love Jesus.

If we had to work our way into heaven, then our works will never be enough for God, who will see our works to be so full of pretense because we have no faith in Jesus Christ.

Only Jesus' ministry work was worthy to please God, because Jesus had no sins.

If we had to work our way into heaven, then we would never get to enter heaven because our works will be a failure to God, who we can only please by faith.

It's always good to work for the Lord, but works along are dead without faith in the Lord Jesus Christ.

If we had to work our way into heaven, then our works would never be enough for God.

Our faith is enough to please God, who gave us His only begotten Son to save us from our sins.

The only worthy thing in the presence of God is that we believe in His Son, Jesus Christ.

Jesus will bless our works to be so true if we are saved in Him.

Will Use the Name of the Lord

There are people who will use the name of the Lord to try to scam people out of their money.

There are people who will use the name of the Lord to try to use people.

There are people who will use the name of the Lord to try to deceive people.

There are people who will use the name of the Lord to try to control people.

There are people who will use the name of the Lord to try to charm people.

There are people who will use the name of the Lord to try to play games on people.

There are people who will use the name of the Lord to try to rob people.

There are people who will use the name of the Lord to try to cheat people.

There are people who will use the name of the Lord to try to flirt with people.

There are people who will use the name of the Lord to try to tear people down.

There are people who will use the name of the Lord in the wrong way for their selfish reasons.

There are people who will use the name of the Lord in the wrong way because they don't love the Lord.

There are people who will use the name of the Lord in the wrong way because they don't have a relationship with the Lord.

There are people who will use the Lord's holy name to try to get you and me to trust them, but the Lord sees them as untrustworthy even to themselves.

Is Too Much

There are people who believe that Jesus is too much for them to think about day after day.

They would rather think about temporary things.

There are people who believe that Jesus is too much for them to talk about day after day.

They would rather talk about who they see, to have no heaven to put them in.

There are people who believe that Jesus is too much for them to worship Him day after day.

They would rather make excuses and worship sinners because they believe that Jesus is too very strict on them about keeping His Commandments.

There are people who believe that Jesus is too much for them to pray to day after day.

They would rather not pray to Jesus because they believe that their prayers are not good enough for Jesus to answer.

There are people who believe that Jesus is too much for them to study about day after day.

They would rather not study at all because they believe that the bible is too complicated and out of date for them to understand who Jesus Christ is.

There are people who believe that Jesus is too much for them to hear about day after day.

They would rather hear the bad news on the TV than hear you and me telling them the good news about Jesus Christ who can save us from our sins and is coming back again to take all of His children to heaven.

We Christians are Supposed to

The sun will shine.

We Christians are supposed to shine our light of living right unto the Lord.

The moonlight will glow all night long.

We Christians are supposed to glow the truth of God's holy word in this dark, sinful world.

The stars will sparkle all night long.

We Christians are supposed to sparkle the mercy of Jesus in this dark, sinful world.

The mountains are high.

We Christians are supposed to be high up in giving testimonies about where Jesus brought us from in this dark, sinful world.

The valley is low.

We Christians are supposed to be low in humility unto Jesus in this dark, sinful world.

The oceans are deep.

We Christians are supposed to be deep in giving Jesus all the glory and praise in this dark, sinful world.

The rivers will flow.

We Christians are supposed to flow the peace of Jesus in this dark, sinful world.

The fire will burn.

We Christians are supposed to be on fire to spread the gospel of Jesus Christ to all the world.

The wind will blow.

We Christians are supposed to blow our witness of Jesus in this dark, sinful world.

The leaves will fall on the ground.

We Christians are supposed to fall down on our knees and pray to Jesus in this dark, sinful world.

The trees will stand tall.

We Christians are supposed to stand tall in not denying Jesus in this dark, sinful world.

The grass will grow.

We Christians are supposed to grow in love for one another through Jesus in this dark, sinful world.

We Christians are supposed to be like Jesus in this dark, sinful world where Jesus once lived without sin to save us from our sins and redeem us back to God.

As We Get Closer and Closer

As we get closer and closer to Jesus coming back again, more and more church folks will turn their backs on Jesus for a high wage salary at their jobs.

As we get closer and closer to Jesus coming back again, more and more church folks will turn their backs on Jesus to live in pleasure.

As we get closer and closer to Jesus coming back again, more and more church folks will turn their backs on Jesus and divorce their spouses.

As we get closer and closer to Jesus coming back again, more and more church folks will turn their backs on Jesus and leave the church.

As we get closer and closer to Jesus coming back again, more and more church folks will turn their backs on Jesus, and live in adultery.

As we get closer and closer to Jesus coming back again, more and more church folks will turn their backs on Jesus to get fame.

As we get closer and closer to Jesus coming back again, more and more church folks will turn their backs on Jesus to get wealth.

As we get closer and closer to Jesus coming back again, more and more church folks will turn their backs on Jesus to get worldly gain.

As we get closer and closer to Jesus coming back again, more and more church folks will turn their backs on Jesus to get a name for themselves.

As we get closer and closer to Jesus coming back again, more and more church folks will turn their backs on Jesus to get success.

As we get closer and closer to Jesus coming back again, more and more church folks will turn their backs on Jesus get accomplishments in this world.

As we get closer and closer to Jesus coming back again, more and more church folks will turn their backs on Jesus and really won't know why.

Let's not turn our backs on Jesus Christ, who will never turn His back on us to save us from our sins that we will be lost in if we turn our backs on Jesus.

The Facts of Life

Many of us had to learn the hard way about the facts of life that our parents didn't teach us about when we were little children.

Many more children will grow up not being taught about the facts of life, and that is a hard reality.

Many of us grew up not being prepared for the hard times in life because of not knowing about the facts of life.

The facts of life are the truth about disappointments that can happen in our lives.

The facts of life are the truth about heartaches that can happen in our lives.

The facts of life are the truth about trouble that can come our way in life.

The facts of life are the truth about mistakes we will make in life.

The facts of life are the truth about making good choices or bad choices in life.

The facts of life are the truth that we will have some enemies in our lives.

The facts of life are a hard reality that many of us adults were not taught when we were little children who could play with each other all day long and have no cares about the facts of life that hid behind the bushes where we couldn't see them laughing at our ignorance.

The facts of life are a hard reality that many little children are not taught today by their parents, because many parents cause their own little children to learn things the hard way, which can be avoided if parents teach their children about the facts of life.

Jesus' parents must have taught Him about the facts of life because Jesus had to grow up like any other little innocent child, even though He was without sin.

The facts of life could not tarnish and break Jesus' perfect life that He lived to give us the victory over the hard reality of the facts of life.

There is More and More of You, O Lord

There is more and more of You, O Lord, to come into my thoughts for me to think on You.

There is more and more of You, O Lord, to come into my words for me to speak about You.

There is more and more of You, O Lord, to come into my heart for me to have motives and intentions about You.

There is more and more of You, O Lord, to come into my actions for me to do Your holy will.

There is more and more of You, O Lord, to come into my life for me to live my renewed life unto You.

There is more and more of You, O Lord, to come into my comings and goings for me to be a witness of You.

There is more and more of You, O Lord, to come into my dreams for me to wake up and share my dreams about You with others.

There is more and more of You, O Lord, to come into my daily activities for me to include You in what I do day after day.

There is more and more of You, O Lord, to come into my eyes for me to see Your love and mercy that chance and luck can't compare to.

There is more and more of You, O Lord, to come into my ears for me to hear more and more truth about You.

There is more and more of You, O Lord, to come into my hands for me to open up the bible and read about You fulfilling God's holy law.

There is more and more of You, O Lord, to come upon my feet for me to walk where You want me to go to represent You.

There is more and more of You, O Lord, to come into my body for me to eat right, drink right, exercise, rest and have good hygiene for Your holy spirit, O Lord, to dwell in day after day.

There is more and more of You, my Lord and Savior Jesus Christ, to come into eternal life that the holy angles know to be true.

They didn't rebel against God, who the fallen angels rebelled against and realized too late that Jesus is above and beyond eternal life that He created to be more and more and forevermore real than life on earth and life in other worlds.

Be In My

Be in my mind, O Lord, for me to think on You day after day.

Be in my heart, O Lord, for me to always love You.

Be in my eyes, O Lord, for me to see Your mercy.

Be in my ears, O Lord, for me to hear Your holy word.

Be in my mouth, O Lord, for me to speak Your holy word in love.

Be in my hands, O Lord, for me to open my bible and study it.

Be in my arms, O Lord, for me to wrap my arms around hurting people in the church and outside the church.

Be in my legs, O Lord, for me to stand on Your promises.

Be in my motives, O Lord, for me to have good reasons.

Be in my intentions, O Lord, for me to do the right things.

Be in my health, O Lord, for me to eat right and exercise my body that is Your temple to dwell in.

Be in my home, O Lord, for me to be Your church in my home.

Be in my vehicle, O Lord, for me to drive safe on the road and to respect other drivers.

Be in my comings and goings, O Lord, for me to represent You wherever I go here and there.

Be in my life, O Lord, for me to live right by example before the world every day that You, O Lord, are a righteous and holy Lord and Savior.

Be in my destiny, O Lord, for me to be saved in You and go with You to heaven when You come back again.

Be in my existence, O Lord, for me to have stars on my crown for winning souls to make it to heaven because You, O Lord, allowed me to still exist today in this world where I can choose to live for You and be a witness of You before others.

The Lord Can Show You and Me

The Lord can show you some good things about me.

The Lord can show me some good things about you.

The Lord can show you some bad things about me.

The Lord can show me some bad things about you.

There is nothing that the Lord can't show to you and me.

The Lord can show you my strength.

The Lord can show you my weakness.

The Lord can show you my motive.

The Lord can show you my intention.

The Lord can show me your strength.

The Lord can show me your motive.

The Lord can show me your intention.

The Lord can show me your strength.

The Lord can show you who I am.

The Lord can show me who you are.

The Lord can show you if I mean what I say.

The Lord can show me if you mean what you say.

The Lord can show you if I am telling you the truth.

The Lord can show you if I am telling you a lie.

The Lord can show me if you are telling me the truth.

The Lord can show me if you are telling me a lie.

The Lord can show you if I am good.

The Lord can show you if I am evil.

The Lord can show me if you are good.

The Lord can show me if you are evil.

There is nothing the Lord can't show to you and me.

The Lord can show you if I am real with you.

The Lord can show you if I am pretending with you.

The Lord can show me if you are real with me.

The Lord can show me if you are pretending with me.

The Lord can show you if I am wise.

The Lord can show you if I am foolish.

The Lord can show me if you are wise.

The Lord can show me if you are foolish.

The Lord can show you if I am intelligent.

The Lord can show you if I am brilliant.

The Lord can show me if you are intelligent.

The Lord can show me if you are brilliant.

The Lord can show you if I am talented.

The Lord can show you if I am gifted.

The Lord can show me if you are talented.

The Lord can show me if you are gifted.

The Lord can show you if I am controlling.

The Lord can show me if you are controlling.

The Lord can show you if I am kind.

The Lord can show me if you are kind.

The Lord can show you if I am talkative.

The Lord can show you if I am quiet.

The Lord can show me if you are talkative.

The Lord can show me if you are quiet.

The Lord can show you if I am friendly.

The Lord can show you if I am trustworthy.

The Lord can show me if you are trustworthy.

The Lord can show you if I love you.

The Lord can show me if you love me.

The Lord can show you if I have common sense.

The Lord can show me if you have common sense.

The Lord can show you if I am a Christian.

The Lord can show me if you are a Christian.

There is nothing that the Lord can't show to you and me.

Survival is Pretty Much About

Survival is pretty much about who is smarter.

Survival is pretty much about who is stronger.

Survival is pretty much about who is more determined.

Survival is pretty much about who is more clever.

Survival is pretty much about who is more encouraging.

Survival is pretty much about who is healthier.

Survival is pretty much about who is more understanding.

Survival is pretty much about who is more intelligent.

Survival is pretty much about who is more talented.

Survival is pretty much about who is more skillful.

Survival is pretty much about who is more loving.

Survival is pretty much about who is more inspiring.

Survival is pretty much about who is more honest.

Survival is pretty much about who is more right.

Survival is pretty much about who is more energetic.

Survival is pretty much about who is more trustworthy.

Survival is pretty much about who is more loyal.

Survival is pretty much about who is more mature.

Survival is pretty much about who is more dependable.

Survival is pretty much about who is more prosperous.

Survival is pretty much about who is more positive.

Survival is pretty much about who is more logical.

Survival is pretty much about who is more victorious.

Survival is pretty much about who is more tactful.

Survival is pretty much about who is more focused.

Survival is pretty much about who is more confident.

Survival is pretty much about who is braver.

Survival is pretty much about who is more in control.

Survival is pretty much about who is more experienced.

Survival is pretty much about who is more giving.

Survival is pretty much about who is friendlier.

Survival is pretty much about who is more spiritual.

Survival is pretty much about who is more powerful.

The poorest people will pretty much survive because God is so good to the poorest of people and supplies all of their needs.

The devil hates to see any human being survive in this world because he would love to destroy every human being, good and evil, if God allows him to.

We can truly thank Jesus Christ for surviving through all of the devil's temptations to give you and me the strength to survive through the devil's temptations that won't overpower us.

Jesus has made a way for us to escape the devil's worst kinds of temptations because Jesus survived through them all to save us from being lost in our sins.

Regretting Something

Regretting something can last for days.

Regretting something can last for weeks.

Regretting something can last for months.

Regretting something can last for a year.

Regretting something can last for a lifetime.

There is nothing good about regretting something that we should not have said.

There is nothing good about regretting something that we should not have done.

Many people have more than a few regrets that stalk them every day.

Regretting something can be hard on us every day.

Regretting something can cause us to be sad.

Regretting something can change someone's life for the worst.

Regretting something has caused many people to lose friends.

Regretting something has caused many people to get sick.

Regretting something has caused many people to take their own lives.

Regretting something is nothing good to stay on our minds.

Many people will seem to regret something that they didn't say.

Many people will seem to regret something that they didn't do.

Many people just don't seem to regret leaving the church.

Many people just don't seem to regret turning their backs on Jesus Christ.

The worst kind of regret is to rebel against the Lord and live a sinful life.

Many people who were once in church don't see that to be the worst kind of regret in their lives.

Many people who go to church don't have any regrets for causing someone to leave the church that Jesus Christ is the head of to separate the wheat from the tares.

Regretting something can be a good thing unto the Lord, who can see our regrets and show us that we must always wait on Him to do what we can't do.

We can surely mess things up and regret it for not waiting on the Lord, who has no regrets for shedding his blood on the cross to save us from our sins.

The Origin Of

God is the origin of life.

God is the origin of heaven.

God is the origin of the angels.

God is the origin of the universe.

God is the origin of this world.

God is the origin of religion.

God is the origin of love.

God is the origin of grace.

God is the origin of truth.

God is the origin of peace.

God is the origin of mercy.

God is the origin of health.

God is the origin of wisdom.

God is the origin of knowledge.

God is the origin of goodness.

God is the origin of joy.

God is the origin of temperance.

God is the origin of worship.

God is the origin of humility.

God is the origin of faith.

God is the origin of hope.

God is the origin of salvation.

God is the origin of gentleness.

God is the origin of kindness.

God is the origin of meekness.

God is the origin of judgment.

God is the origin of justice.

God is the origin of reverence.

God is the origin of trust.

God is the origin of power.

God is the origin of words.

God is the origin of actions.

God is the origin of obedience.

God is the origin of beauty.

God is the origin of strength.

God is the origin of wealth.

God is the origin of respect.

God is the origin of righteousness.

God is the origin of holiness.

God is the origin of perfection.

God is the origin of time.

The devil is the origin of sin.

The devil is the origin of death.

The devil is the origin of the grave.

The devil is the origin of hate.

The devil is the origin of injustice.

The devil is the origin of slavery.

The devil is the origin of violence.

The devil is the origin of abuse.

The devil is the origin of lies.

The devil is the origin of war.

The devil is the origin of envy.

The devil is the origin of disobedience.

The devil is the origin of murder.

The devil is the origin of covetousness.

The devil is the origin of gossip.

The devil is the origin of strife.

The devil is the origin of pretense.

The devil is the origin of deception.

The devil is the origin of magic.

The devil is the origin of spiritualism.

The devil is the origin of evil.

The devil is the origin of wickedness.

The devil is the origin of lust.

The devil is the origin of adultery.

The devil is the origin of fornication.

God is the origin of healing.

God is the origin of all good things.

God is the origin of all existence seen and unseen.

Falsely Accused

Many people get falsely accused because of the color of their skin.

Many people get falsely accused because they look different.

Many people get falsely accused because they talk different.

Many people get falsely accused because they walk different.

Many people get falsely accused because they dress different.

Many people get falsely accused because they are poor.

Many people get falsely accused because they act different.

Many people get falsely accused for being at the wrong place.

Many people get falsely accused because they have no witnesses.

Many people get falsely accused because of someone being jealous of them.

Many people get falsely accused because of someone being envious of them.

Many people get falsely accused because of someone hating them.

Many people get falsely accused for no good reason at all.

Many people get falsely accused for helping someone.

Many people get falsely accused for being kind to someone.

We Christians get falsely accused by the devil every day.

We Christians get falsely accused by the devil's human agents.

We Christians get falsely accused by so-called Christians.

Jesus was falsely accused by the religious leaders and Pharisees when He lived on earth without sin.

They falsely accused Jesus of being the devil.

They falsely accused Jesus of being a blasphemer.

Many people are falsely accusing Jesus today by saying that Jesus was only a prophet and not the Son of God.

If You are Living in Sin

No matter how rich you are, if you are living in sin you will be lost in your sins that Jesus never committed against God for you and me to be saved in Him.

No matter how genius you are, if you are living in sin you will be lost in your sins that Jesus became on the cross and died on the cross to set you and me free from the bondage of sin.

No matter how famous you are, if you are living in sin you will be lost in your sins that Jesus overcame in this world where He humbled Himself even unto death.

No matter how great you are, if you are living in sin you will be lost in your sins that Jesus will cast into the deepest sea if you confess and repent of those sins unto Jesus Christ.

No matter how much you go to church, if you are living in sin you will be lost in your sins that Jesus can cleanse you and me from through His precious blood that was shed on the cross.

No matter how many bible scriptures you know, if you are living in sin you will be lost in your sins that Jesus will save you from if you deny yourself and pick up your cross and follow Jesus.

No matter how many spiritual gifts you have in the church, if you are living in sin you will be lost in your sins that Jesus hates but He loves your soul.

No matter how long you have been in the church, if you are living in sin you will be lost in your sins that Jesus cast out of heaven so long ago, before you were born into this old world.

Loneliest

Beautiful women can be some of the loneliest people in this world because many men will only want them for their beauty and not for their brains.

Great people can be some of the loneliest people in this world because many people will only look at them for their greatness and not for who they are, being a human being like you and me.

Rich people can be some of the loneliest people in this world because many people will only look at them for being rich and not for being a normal person who needs good friends.

Genius people can be some of the loneliest people in this world because many people will only look at them as being nerds who they can't talk to and understand on their level of average intelligence.

We true Christians can be the loneliest people in this world because the people of the world will only look at us as strange people because we believe in Jesus Christ, but they don't mind if we pray for them if they are on their death bed and hoping for a miracle so they can live to see more years.

Jesus must have been the loneliest man who ever lived in this world.

Jesus lived without sin and no one else could relate to that because everyone else around him had sins to confess and repent of unto God.

With His Smooth Temptations

The devil will come to you and me with his smooth temptations anytime and anywhere.

The devil is smooth with his temptations, so much more than a little bit.

The devil will try his best to cause you and me to sin against God with our eyes.

The devil will try his best to cause you and me to sin against God with our hands.

The devil will try his best to cause you and me to sin against God with our feet.

The devil will try his best to cause you and me to sin against God with our thoughts.

The devil will try his best to cause you and me to sin against God with our words.

The devil will try his best to cause you and me to sin against God with our bodies.

The devil will come to you and me with his smooth temptations that will catch us off guard if we don't pray to the Lord Jesus Christ to help us to represent Him wherever we go.

Staying prayed up unto the Lord will surely protect us from giving into the devil's smooth temptations that can also come into the church.

The devil will come to you and me with his smooth temptations that are not so transparent right away in our eyesight.

The devil will come to you and me with his smooth temptations that can sneak right up on us anytime and anywhere in the day and night.

Staying in prayer is our power to resist the devil's smooth and rough temptations.

It's usually the devil's smooth temptations that we don't often see, and they trap us like a fly landing down into a Venus fly trap.

Thanks to Jesus Christ, the devil can't tempt us with more than what we can bear with his smooth and rough temptations that we can escape from by keeping our eyes on Jesus Christ, who will give us the strength to resist the devil's temptations anytime and anywhere we go.

It's Not Always Easy To

It's not always easy to love everybody in our family.

We surely need the Lord to help us to love everybody in our family.

Some of our family can sometimes be hard to talk to and get along with.

It's not always easy to love everybody in our neighborhood.

We surely need the Lord to help us to love everybody in our neighborhood.

Some people in our neighborhood can be hard to get to know because they keep their distance like we might take something away from them.

We surely need the Lord to help us to love everybody in our family.

It's not always easy to love everybody on the job.

We surely need the Lord to help us to love everybody on the job.

Some people on the job just don't care anything about us, and act as if they are the only ones working on the job.

It's not always easy to love everybody in this world.

We surely need the Lord to help us to love everybody in this world.

So many people are so evil and will kill us if they get the chance and not care at all if we are a Christian.

It's not always easy to love everybody in the church.

We surely need the Lord to help us to love everybody in the church.

Some people in the church can be hard to love because they will shut you and me out of their lives like we are a stray dog to them.

It's not always easy to love and obey Jesus Christ.

We surely need Jesus to help us to love Him.

The devil will always try his best to tempt us to sin against Jesus, who will give us His holy spirit no matter how much we don't deserve Jesus to save us from our sins.

There Won't Be

There won't be any people in heaven who hold grudges.

There won't be any people in heaven who are proud.

There won't be any people in heaven who are abusers.

There won't be any people in heaven who are selfish.

There won't be any people in heaven who tell lies.

There won't be any people in heaven who are fornicators.

There won't be any people in heaven who are murderers.

There won't be any people in heaven who are thieves.

There won't be any people in heaven who are users.

There won't be any people in heaven who are prostituting.

There won't be any people in heaven who are homosexuals.

There won't be any people in heaven who are rapists.

There won't be any people in heaven who are greedy for worldly gain.

There won't be any people in heaven who are gossipers.

There won't be any people in heaven who are foolish.

There won't be any people in heaven who are lazy.

There won't be any people in heaven who are deceptive.

There won't be any people in heaven who are jokesters.

There won't be any people in heaven who lust.

There won't be any people in heaven who don't confess and repent of their sins unto Jesus Christ.

There won't be any people in heaven who don't believe in Jesus Christ.

There won't be any people in heaven who are hypocrites.

There won't be any people in heaven who turn their backs on Jesus.

There won't be any people in heaven who are playing church.

There won't be any people in heaven who are playing God.

God's Blessings

We should never take God's blessings for granted.

It's a blessing to have eyes to see.

It's a blessing to have ears to hear.

It's a blessing to have hands to hold.

It's a blessing to have legs and feet to walk.

What we go through in our lives is nothing compared to God blessing us.

There are people who can't see.

There are people who can't hear.

There are people who can't walk.

But, the Lord still blesses them with life to know that they are alive and can thank God that they are not dead in the grave.

We should never take God's blessings for granted.

It's a blessing to have a mind to make choices, whether we're in our right mind or not in our right mind.

Animals and all the other creatures that God created don't have a mind to make choices.

We human beings are so very blessed that God created us in His own image.

God didn't have to do that.

We should never take God's blessings for granted no matter what bad things we go through in our lives, because as long as God gives us life we are so blessed to be in His image.

We can never be too bad off that God can't bless us in some kind of way.

We should never take God's blessings for granted, but many people do take this for granted every day.

They believe they are self-made and will claim God has nothing to do with them being successful in life.

No Matter How Much You Tell People

No matter how much you tell people the truth about God's holy word, many people just don't want to change from their selfish ways.

No matter how much you tell people the truth about God's holy word, many people just don't want to believe you.

No matter how much you tell people the truth about God's holy word, many people just don't want to give up their traditional ways of doing their own will.

No matter how much you tell people the truth about God's holy word, many people just don't want to confess of their sins and repent.

No matter how much you tell people the truth about God's holy word, many people just don't want to deny self and pick up their crosses and follow Jesus Christ.

No matter how much you tell people the truth about God's holy word, many people just don't want to believe in Jesus Christ.

No matter how much you tell people the truth about God's holy word, many people just don't want to go to church.

No matter how much you tell people the truth about God's holy word, many people just don't want to read the bible.

No matter how much you tell people the truth about God's holy word, many people just don't want to live right by God's holy word.

You Can't Always

You can't always take people's word for what they tell you because they might be telling you a lie.

You can't always be right about what you think about the people you know because those people might not be honest with you about everything.

You can't always be right about what you say about the people you know because those people might show you something different about themselves.

You can't always be right about what you say about anyone because only the Lord knows the whole heart beyond the outward appearance.

You can't always be right about what you do because you are not perfect and can't do everything right.

You can't always know the people you live with because they may show you something different about themselves.

If you are a Christian, you can't always know the Lord Jesus Christ because Jesus can show you something good and different about Him to cause you to be so amazed that He answered your prayers.

If you are a Christian, you can't always know the Lord Jesus Christ because Jesus can show you something good and different about Him as you go through your trials and must wait on Him to bring you through.

You can truly know that Jesus is for you, even though you can't always know God who can sometimes work in mysterious ways.

Don't Want to Have Anything to do With

There are people who don't want to have anything to do with you if you don't let them use you.

There are people who don't want to have anything to do with you if you don't kiss up to them.

There are people who don't want to have anything to do with you if you don't worship them.

There are people who don't want to have anything to do with you if you look different from them.

There are people who don't want to have anything to do with you if you don't laugh at their jokes.

There are people who don't want to have anything to do with you if you tell them the truth about their bad ways.

There are people who don't want to have anything to do with you if you move up in life and seem to be a threat to them.

There are people who don't want to have anything to do with you if you are good and not bad like them.

Back in the bible days, there were people who didn't want to have anything to do with Jesus because He always spoke the truth in love that they couldn't handle.

There were people who didn't want to have anything to do with Jesus because He didn't use His power to overthrow the Roman government.

Back in the bible days, there were people who didn't want to have anything to do with Jesus because He loved everybody the same, no matter the color of their skin.

Back in the bible days, there were people who didn't want to have anything to do with Jesus because He performed miracles that they couldn't do.

Back in the bible days, there were people who didn't want to have anything to do with Jesus because they were envious of Him.

Back in the bible days, there were people who didn't want to have anything to do with Jesus because He claimed to be the Son of God.

Anybody Can Be

Anybody can be unfaithful to their spouse if they don't live their lives unto Jesus.

Anybody can mess things up if they don't live their lives unto Jesus.

Anybody can tell lies if they don't live their lives unto Jesus.

Anybody can be greedy for worldly gain if they don't live their lives unto Jesus.

Anybody can be proud if they don't live their lives unto Jesus.

Anybody can be bad if they don't live their lives unto Jesus.

Anybody can be selfish if they don't live their lives unto Jesus.

Anybody can shorten their own lives if they don't live their lives unto Jesus.

Anybody can be delusional if they don't live their lives unto Jesus.

Anybody can be deceptive if they don't live their lives unto Jesus.

Anybody can be ignorant if they don't live their lives unto Jesus.

Anybody can be untrustworthy if they don't live their lives unto Jesus.

Anybody can be in bondage if they don't live their lives unto Jesus.

Anybody can be envious if they don't live their lives unto Jesus.

Anybody can be a wreck if they don't live their lives unto Jesus.

Anybody can be discouraging if they don't live their lives unto Jesus.

Anybody can steal if they don't live their lives unto Jesus.

Anybody can kill if they don't live their lives unto Jesus.

Anybody can fail if they don't live their lives unto Jesus.

Anybody can live in sin if they don't live their lives unto Jesus.

Living our lives unto Jesus can surely make the devil tremble.

Living our lives unto Jesus can surely make the evil flee from us.

Living our lives unto Jesus will surely secure our destiny to heaven.

Anybody can be insecure if they don't live their lives unto Jesus.

Anybody can be just like the devil if they don't live their lives unto Jesus Christ, who defeated the devil when He rose from the grave with power and victory over death.

It was You, Lord Jesus

It was You, Lord Jesus, who created the heavens and earth.

It was You, Lord Jesus, who created all the angels

It was You, Lord Jesus, who created other worlds.

It was You, Lord Jesus, who created all the animals.

It was You, Lord Jesus, who created the sun, moon and stars.

It was You, Lord Jesus, who created Adam and Eve.

It was You, Lord Jesus, who told Noah to build an ark.

It was You, Lord Jesus, who commanded the animals to get in the ark.

It was You, Lord Jesus, who talked to Moses in the burning bush.

It was You, Lord Jesus, who stopped Abraham from killing his son Isaac.

It was You, Lord Jesus, who Jacob wrestled with.

It was You, Lord Jesus, who parted the Red Sea.

It was You, Lord Jesus, who parted the Jordan River.

It was You, Lord Jesus, who knocked down the Jericho walls.

It was You, Lord Jesus, who protected Daniel in the lion's den.

It was You, Lord Jesus, who shut the lion's mouth in the lion's den.

It was You, Lord Jesus, who was in the furnace fire with the three Hebrew boys.

It was You, Lord Jesus, who appeared before Saul in a bright light and spoke to him when he was on his way to Damascus to persecute the Christians.

It was You, Lord Jesus, who changed Saul's name to Paul.

It was You, Lord Jesus, who was Michael the archangel fighting against Lucifer and cast him and his angels out of heaven.

It was You, Lord Jesus, who hid Moses' body away from the devil before You took him to heaven.

It was You, Lord Jesus, who created all things.

It was You, Lord Jesus, who set Ezekiel in the middle of the valley of dry bones where You, O Lord, gave life again to a vast army.

Conspiracy is of the Devil

One nation can conspire against another nation to bring it down to ruin.

Conspiracy can come in all kinds of ways.

Smuggling drugs in a nation is a conspiracy to kill many people and weaken a nation.

Cyberattacks against a nation are a conspiracy to bankrupt that nation and make it fall into ruin.

Deadly viruses coming into a nation is a conspiracy to make many people sick and kill them to discourage a nation.

Spying on a nation is a conspiracy to steal very vital information from a nation to make that nation vulnerable.

Conspiracy is of the devil, who has his human agents to conspire especially against God's holy children.

The devil and his human agents will conspire against you and me and try to make us look like hypocrites for living right unto the Lord.

The devil also has human agents in the church where so-called Christians will not live right by God's holy word and will cause you and me to look bad for not doing the wrong things that they are doing.

Conspiracy is nothing new today.

Lucifer had conspired against God in heaven, where he caused one-third of the angels in heaven to rebel against God.

The Pharisees and religious leaders conspired against Jesus to try to trap Him into saying something wrong and doing something wrong.

Anyone who loves to conspire is of the devil.

Conspiring against a nation is all about trying to find a way to gain power and control over a nation.

Many people will conspire against people in their own family, especially when it comes to trying to get control of a lot of money.

Conspiracy had no victory over the Lord Jesus Christ, who saw through all of His enemies' conspiracies when He lived here on earth without sin.

Will Pass Away One Day

Everything in this world will pass away one day when the Lord will create a new heaven and a new earth.

All of the houses will pass away one day.

All of the buildings will pass away one day.

All of the trucks will pass away one day.

All of the cars will pass away one day.

All of the airplanes will pass away one day.

All of the rockets will pass away one day.

All of the phones will pass away one day.

All of the computers will pass away one day.

All of the jewelry will pass away one day.

All of the banks will pass away one day.

All of the funeral homes will pass away one day.

All of the hospitals will pass away one day.

All of the oceans will pass away one day.

All of the ships will pass away one day.

All of the boats will pass away one day.

All of the military will pass away one day.

All of the governments will pass away one day.

Everything in this world will pass away one day when Jesus Christ comes back again.

All of the demons will pass away one day.

All of the wicked will pass away one day.

All of hell will pass away one day.

All of the rebellion against God will pass away one day.

All of this sinful world will pass away one day.

The devil will pass away one day.

All who are saved in Jesus Christ will not pass away.

Death will pass away one day.

All kinds of evilness will pass away one day.

God's love will never pass away.

The price that Jesus paid for us to be saved in Him will never pass away.

All of the trains will pass away one day.

All of the buses will pass away one day.

All of the schools will pass away one day.

All of the colleges will pass away one day.

All of the universities will pass away one day.

Jesus will create a new heaven and new earth one day after he destroys this old, sinful world along with everything in it.

Everything that human beings created in this world will be destroyed and pass away one day.

Only the righteous children of God will live in the new heaven and new earth with Jesus one day.

All of the restaurants will pass away one day.

All of the businesses will pass away one day.

All of the money in this world will pass away one day.

Everything in this world will pass away one day and Jesus Christ will create a new heaven and new earth for all of His children to live in forever and ever.

Will Think of Ways

Many rich people will think of ways to get richer.

Many poor people will think of ways to survive.

Many athletes will think of ways to be a better athlete.

Many educated people will think of ways to get more knowledge.

Many skillful people will think of ways to sharpen their skills.

Many entertainers will think of ways to entertain people.

Many movie stars will think of ways to move more people's hearts.

Many criminals will think of ways to commit more crimes.

Many politicians will think of ways to get more votes.

Many lawyers will think of ways to win more court cases.

Many news reporters will think of ways to report more news.

Many scam artists will think of ways to scam more people.

A few married couples will think of ways to keep their marriage together.

Many soldiers will think of ways to be a better soldier.

A few church folks will think of ways to encourage their brothers and sisters in the Lord.

A few church folks will think of ways to win souls to the Lord.

A few church folks will think of ways to spread the gospel of Jesus Christ.

A few church folks will think of ways to help their spiritual brothers and sisters hold onto the Lord.

A few church folks will think of ways to esteem their spiritual brothers and sisters in the Lord.

A few church folks will think of ways to meet people where they are on their level to help them give their hearts to Jesus.

We Would Rather Look at and Talk About

We would rather look at and talk about someone else's flaws than look at and talk about our own flaws.

We would rather look at and talk about someone else's mistakes than look at and talk about our own mistakes.

We would rather look at and talk about someone else's problems than look at and talk about our own problems.

We would rather look at and talk about someone else's downfalls than look at and talk about our own downfalls.

We would rather look at and talk about someone else's bad behavior than look at and talk about our own bad behavior.

We would rather look at and talk about someone else's wrongdoings than look at and talk about our own wrongdoings.

We would rather look at and talk about someone else's disappointments than look at and talk about our own disappointments.

We would rather look at and talk about someone else's misfortunes than look at and talk about our own misfortunes.

We would rather look at and talk about someone else's defeats than look at and talk about our own defeats.

We would rather look at and talk about someone else's distress than look at and talk about our own distress.

We would rather look at and talk about someone else's imperfections than look at and talk about our own imperfections.

We would rather look at and talk about someone else's sins than look at and talk about our own sins.

When Jesus Christ lived here on earth without sin, He never looked at and talked about sinners being doomed to go to hell because Jesus came to this world to save sinners like you and me from our sins and not to condemn us in our sins.

Age Doesn't Matter

Age doesn't matter for the Lord to use you.

Age doesn't matter for the Lord to bless you real good.

Age doesn't matter for the Lord to open a door for you.

Age doesn't matter for the Lord to make you great

Age doesn't matter for the Lord to prosper you.

Age doesn't matter for the Lord to give you wisdom.

Age doesn't matter for the Lord to give you knowledge.

Age doesn't matter for the Lord to give you courage.

Age doesn't matter for the Lord to give you His favor.

Age doesn't matter for the Lord to be for you.

Age doesn't matter for the Lord to give you discernment.

Age doesn't matter for the Lord to give you joy.

Age doesn't matter for the Lord to give you peace of mind.

The only difference in age is that the Lord can use you a lot more if you are young and energetic.

Age doesn't matter for the Lord to humble you.

Age doesn't matter for the Lord to chastise you.

Age doesn't matter for the Lord to strengthen you.

Age doesn't matter for the Lord to give you spiritual gifts.

Age doesn't matter for the Lord to bless your health.

Age doesn't matter for the Lord to protect you.

Age doesn't matter for the Lord to open the windows of heaven and pour out blessings upon you that there shall not be room enough to receive.

Age doesn't matter for the Lord to allow you to be a blessing to others.

Age doesn't matter for the Lord to save you from your sins.

Age doesn't matter for the Lord to heal you.

Age doesn't matter for the Lord to bless you to live to see another day or another year.

Age doesn't matter for the Lord to love you.

Age doesn't matter for the Lord to direct your path.

The Lord shows no respect of age to be His church.

The Lord Can Open Doors

The Lord can open doors that we can't ever imagine because they are so far beyond what our minds can comprehend.

We just don't know when the Lord will open a door for us to walk through.

The Lord can open a door that's been locked for a long time.

The Lord can open doors for you and me while we sleep and dream away in the night.

The Lord can open doors for you and me to be a witness of Him before others.

We can open the front door of our house and see the same old things.

We can open the back door of our house and see the same old things.

When the Lord opens a door for us, we will surely see something new that will surely get our full attention.

The doors that the Lord opens are so much bigger than the doors to our houses that thieves can kick down.

The Lord can also close a door that no one can open no matter how skillful he may be.

The Lord can open a door for you and me who must walk through it with thankfulness and joy unto the Lord Jesus Christ.

The Lord is always on time to open doors for you and me who the Lord knows to be ready to walk through to give Him all the glory and praise.

The Lord can open doors that people can shut in our faces.

The Lord can open spiritual doors and material doors for you and me to walk through with humility unto the Lord who can surprise us when we least expect for Him to open doors for us.

Can't Do More
than What God Allows

You and I can't do more than what God allows us to do.

If you go very far in your life, it's because God allowed you to go very far in your life.

If you are educated, it's because God allowed you to be educated.

If you are rich, it's because God allowed you to be rich.

If you are skillful, it's because God allowed you to be skillful in what you do.

If you are talented, it's because God allowed you to be very talented.

If you are beautiful, it's because God allowed you to be beautiful.

You and I can't do more than what God allows us to do.

The Pharisees couldn't do more to Jesus than what Jesus allowed them to do.

The devil couldn't do more to Jesus than what Jesus allowed the devil to do.

The devil can't do more than what God allows the devil to do.

No man can do more than what God allows him to do.

No woman can do more than what God allows her to do.

No hurricane can do more damage than what God allows it to do.

No tornado can do more damage than what God allows it to do.

No earthquake can do more damage than what God allows it to do.

No flood can do more damage than what God allows it to do.

No wildfire can do more damage than what God allows it to do.

No disease can do more ill than what God allows it to do.

No virus can do more ill than what God allows it to do.

No heatwave can do more scorching than what God allows it to do.

No winter season can do more freezing cold than what God allows it to do.

The devil can't tempt you and me with more than what God allows him to tempt us with.

Whatever goes on in this world, good or bad, won't be more than what God allows it to be.

God is in control of all things and He decides what He will allow or not allow, including the devil taking our life whether we are good or bad.

God is in control of all things and He decides what He will allow or not allow, including whether you and I live a long life, because God always knows what is best for us.

The devil couldn't do more to Job than what God allowed him to do.

No one in this world can do more than what God allows.

Just because God allows evil to get worse and worse doesn't mean that God is not in control.

God cannot lie in His holy word, and He tells us that in these last days there will be perilous times.

The devil can't do more than what God allows him to do to you and me, even if we must face death — that can't separate us from God giving us eternal life in His Son, Jesus Christ.

There is Nothing God Can't Do

If God can speak the heavens and earth into existence, then there is nothing that God can't do for you and me.

If God can speak the sun, moon and stars into existence, then there is nothing that God can't do for you and me.

If God can speak nature into existence, then there is nothing that God can't do for you and me.

If God can speak the animals into existence, then there is nothing that God can't do for you and me.

If God can mold and shape a man and woman into His image, then there is nothing that God can't do for you and me.

If God can speak through a burning bush, then there is nothing that God can't do for you and me.

If God can make food fall from the sky, then there is nothing that God can't do for you and me.

If God can part the Red Sea, then there is nothing that God can't do for you and me.

If God can part the Jordan River, then there is nothing that God can't do for you and me.

If God can make fire come from the sky, then there is nothing that God can't do for you and me.

If God can shut the lion's mouth, then there is nothing that God can't do for you and me.

If God can give a man the strength to kill a thousand men with a jawbone, then there is nothing that God can't do for you and me.

If God can give a man the wisdom to be the richest man in the world, then there is nothing that God can't do for you and me.

If God can make a virgin woman pregnant then there is nothing that God can't do for you and me.

If God can give His only begotten Son to save us from our sins, then there is nothing that God can't do for you and me.

There were other miraculous things that God did back in the bible days.

God is still doing miraculous things today for you and me to know that there is nothing that God can't do for you and me through His Son, Jesus Christ, who is also God who was made flesh.

We Take a Chance with Our Lives

We take a chance with our lives by living in our houses.

We don't know if the ground will cave in beneath our houses.

We take a chance with our lives when we leave our houses.

We don't know if something will fall on us out of the sky.

We take a chance with our lives when we drive on the roads.

We don't know if another driver will crash into us.

We take a chance with our lives when we drive on a bridge.

We don't know if the bridge will collapse.

We take a chance with our lives when we go to the store.

We don't know if a mass shooter will walk in the store and start shooting everybody.

We take a chance with our lives when we fall asleep.

We don't know if we will wake up again.

We take a chance with our lives even when we go to church.

We don't know if someone will walk in the church and start shooting.

We take a chance with our lives wherever we may go.

We don't know what kind of trouble will come our way.

We take a chance with our lives every day in this sinful world where it's so easy to get killed.

We take a chance with our lives, but Jesus Christ is our only hope to spare our lives for us to see another day.

We take a chance with our lives, but Jesus is our only real, true protection to command our guardian angels to secure our lives.

We take a chance with our lives without always realizing that the devil is always seeking anyone who he can devour.

We take a chance with our lives if we do our own will.

God's will can truly prolong our lives far beyond the chance that we take with our lives day after day.

The Christian Life

The Christian life has its mountaintop experiences.

The Christian life has its deep valley experiences.

The Christian life has its good days.

The Christian life has its bad days.

The Christian life has its grief.

The Christian life has its joy.

The Christian life has its encouragements.

The Christian life has its discouragements.

The Christian life has its ups.

The Christian life has its downs.

The Christian life has its bible truth.

The Christian life has its disappointments

The Christian life has its hardships.

The Christian life has its victories.

The Christian life has its faith in Jesus Christ

The Christian life has its hope in Jesus Christ.

The Christian life has its love for Jesus.

The Christian life has its love for everybody.

The Christian life has its love for justice.

The Christian life has its love for peace.

The Christian life has its love for equality.

The Christian life has its love for education.

The Christian life has its wolves in sheep's clothing.

The Christian life has its unity.

The Christian life has its divisions.

The Christian life has its true children on God.

The Christian Life has its hypocrites.

The Christian life has its improvements.

The Christian life has its achievements.

The Christian life has its spiritual highs.

The Christian life has its spiritual lows.

The Christian life has its youth.

The Christian life has its vigor.

The Christian life has its pure heart.

The Christian life has its wealth.

The Christian life has its poverty.

The Christian life has its army of God.

The Christian life has its good benefits.

The Christian life has its good support.

The Christian life has its good news.

The Christian life has its enemies.

The Christian life has its strong foundation.

The Christian life has its boldness.

The Christian life has its holy people.

The Christian life has its righteous people.

The Christian life has its modest apparel.

The Christian life has its wise people.

The Christian life has its humble people.

The Christian life has its genius people.

The Christian life has its obedient people.

The Christian life has its beauty queens.

The Christian life has its persecutions.

The Christian life has its spiritual family.

The Christian life has its storms.

The Christian life has its rainbows.

The Christian life has its sunshine.

The Christian life has its mysteries.

The Christian life has its crisis.

The Christian life has its skillful people.

The Christian life has its giving people.

The Christian life has its talented people.

The Christian life has its heroic people.

The Christian life has its selfless people.

The Christian life has its martyr people.

The Christian life has its oppressed people.

The Christian life has its temperate people.

The Christian life has its kind people.

The Christian life has its gentle people.

The Christian life has its perseverant people.

The Christian life has its discerning people.

The Christian life has its healing people.

The Christian life has its spiritual born-again people in Jesus Christ.

The Christian life has its advancements to enter into heaven through Jesus Christ, regardless of life difficulties that the devil brings upon every Christian for being saved in Jesus Christ.

The Christian life has its assurance in Jesus Christ, no matter how useless we may feel in the church.

The Christian life has a bright, radiant spiritual light to shine through the darkest soul with the truth of God's holy word that can set the darkest soul free from the devil's lies.

Don't Come Close To

The actors in the Christian movies and miniseries don't come close to portraying the real Adam and Eve.

The actors in the Christian movies and miniseries don't come close to portraying the real Cain and Abel.

The actors in the Christian movies and miniseries don't come close to portraying the real Noah.

The actors in the Christian movies and miniseries don't come close to portraying the real Abraham and Sarah

The actors in the Christian movies and miniseries don't come close to portraying the real Jacob, Leah and Rachel.

The actors in the Christian movies and miniseries don't come close to portraying the real Joseph.

The actors in the Christian movies and miniseries don't come close to portraying the real Zipporah.

The actors in the Christian movies and miniseries don't come close to portraying the real Joshua.

The actors in the Christian movies and miniseries don't come close to portraying the real Rahab.

The actors in the Christian movies and miniseries don't come close to portraying the real Daniel and three Hebrew boys.

The actors in the Christian movies and miniseries don't come close to portraying the real John the Baptist.

The actors in the Christian movies and miniseries don't come close to portraying the real mother of Jesus.

The actors in the Christian movies and miniseries don't come close to portraying the real disciples of Jesus.

The actors in the Christian movies and miniseries don't come close to portraying the real Mary Magdalene.

The actors in the Christian movies and miniseries don't come close to portraying the real Pharisees and Roman soldiers.

The actors in the Christian movies and miniseries don't come close to portraying the real devil.

The actors in the Christian movies and miniseries don't come close to portraying the real Jesus Christ.

Even though the actors don't come close to portraying the people in the bible, the Lord can use them to win souls to Him.

Even though the actors don't come close to portraying the real people in the bible, they can be a good influence on you and me and leave a good impression on you and me to live right unto Jesus who will come back again and raise all the righteous people in the bible from the grave to join you and me in going with Jesus back to heaven where there will be no need to portray anyone.

The Best Good News to Spread

The best good news to spread is the gospel of Jesus Christ in our homes.

The best good news to spread is the gospel of Jesus Christ in our neighborhoods.

The best good news to spread is the gospel of Jesus Christ in our states.

The best good news to spread is the gospel of Jesus Christ in our cities.

The best good news to spread is the gospel of Jesus Christ in our nation.

The best good news to spread is the gospel of Jesus Christ in our all around the world.

The best good news to spread is the gospel of Jesus Christ in our sermons.

The best good news to spread is the gospel of Jesus Christ in our bible school lessons.

The best good news to spread is the gospel of Jesus Christ in our songs.

The best good news to spread is the gospel of Jesus Christ in our poetry.

The best good news to spread is the gospel of Jesus Christ in our actions.

The best good news to spread will not go void to reach around the world before Jesus comes back again.

The best good news to spread will not go void in every born-again believer in Jesus Christ.

The best good news to spread is broadcast throughout the heavens and other worlds to see repentant souls turning to Jesus, who left all His riches in heaven to come to this dark and sinful world to save us sinners from our sins.

The best good news to spread is preparing the true church to be ready to see Jesus Christ coming back again on the clouds of glory to take His true church bride back to heaven with Him one day soon.

The best good news to spread is the gospel of Jesus Christ from the tips of our tongues every day.

The best good news to spread is the gospel of Jesus Christ from the tips of our body language every day that we live.

Being Content is Being Rich In

Being content is being rich in accepting the little things that we have.

Being content is being thankful for the little things that we have.

Being content is being rich in not being greedy for worldly gain.

Being content is being rich in not worrying about what we don't have.

Being content is being rich in happiness about the Lord supplying all of our needs.

Being content is being rich in not wanting what we don't need.

Being content is being rich in giving what little we have to others who are in need.

Being content is being rich in not wanting what others have.

Being content is being rich in working for the Lord without wanting to achieve any recognition.

Being content is being rich in accepting the spiritual gifts the Lord has given to you to not compare yourself with others.

Being content is being rich in being who the Lord called you to be, and that won't be anything that isn't like Him.

O Lord, You Know

O Lord, You know what I will say before I say it.

O Lord, You know what I will see before I see it.

O Lord, You know what I will hear before I hear it.

O Lord, You know what I will feel before I feel it.

O Lord, You know what I will touch before I touch it.

O Lord, You know what I will eat before I eat it.

O Lord, You know what I will drink before I drink it.

O Lord, You know what clothes I will wear before I wear them.

O Lord, You know where I will go before I go there.

O Lord, You know what I will think before I think it.

O Lord, You know what I will smell before I smell it.

O Lord, You know what I will do before I do it.

O Lord, there is nothing that You don't know about me.

O Lord, You know my motives before I know them.

O Lord, You know all of my past life.

O Lord, You know all of my present life.

O Lord, You know all of my future life.

O Lord, You know what choice I will make before I make it.

O Lord, You know my heart before I do anything.

O Lord, You know my life before I see taking me far or nowhere in life.

O Lord, You know my destiny before I make my choices.

O Lord, You know me completely before I lay down to sleep and dream about things You know before I dream it.

Many People

Many people don't know better and don't want to know better to live better.

Many people love to read hardcore books, whether they're non-fiction or fiction.

Many people love to boast about themselves.

Many people love to tell lies.

Many people love to gossip.

Many people love to sing.

Many people love to dance.

Many people love to use people.

Many people love to eat a lot of food.

Many people love to drink alcohol.

Many people love to smoke cigarettes.

Many people love to use drugs.

Many people love to commit crimes.

Many people love to work too much.

Many people talk too much.

Many people are unfaithful to their spouses.

Many people are prejudiced.

Many people are judgmental.

Many people won't think before they talk.

Many people are mean.

Many people are hateful.

Many people are deceivers.

Many people are educated.

Many people are sick.

Many people are poor.

Many people are rich.

Many people were born out of wedlock.

Many people are divorced.

Many people are married.

Many people are incontinent.

Many people are weak-minded.

Many people are violent.

Many people are disrespectful.

Many people are impolite.

Many people are rude.

Many people are proud.

Many people are self-centered.

Many people are ignorant.

Many people are stupid.

Many people are smart.

Many people are serious.

Many people are funny.

Many people love to party.

Many people are wild.

Many people are young.

Many people are middle-aged.

Many church people are lost in their sins.

Many church people don't have a relationship with Jesus Christ.

Many church people are playing church.

Many church people are not spiritually awake.

Many church people don't read their bibles.

Many church people don't give testimonies about what Jesus brought them through.

Many church people don't give God their best with their spiritual gifts that God has given to them.

Many church people are tares.

Many church people will not go to heaven when Jesus Christ comes back again.

Many church people don't take God's word seriously.

Many church people don't take Jesus serious and love Jesus and keep His Commandments.

Perfect

Many people want to talk perfect.

Many people want to walk perfect.

Many people want to look perfect.

Many people want to act perfect.

Many people want to drive perfect.

Many people want to run perfect.

Many people want to write a perfect book.

Many people want to sing perfect.

Many people want to dance perfect.

Many people want to work perfect.

Many people want to dress perfect.

Many people want to do everything perfect.

Many people come very close to perfection in the words they say.

Many people come very close to perfection in the things they do.

Even many criminals want to commit the perfect crime.

No one is perfect and will say every word perfectly.

No one is perfect and will do everything perfectly.

Only Jesus Christ was perfect to have no sins when He lived here on earth.

Many people want perfect health.

Many people want a perfect body.

Many people want a perfect mind.

Only Jesus Christ was perfect to have no sins to save us from our sins.

We are not perfect because we have sins to confess and repent of unto Jesus Christ.

We can never be perfect in our own way of living.

If you are a new creature in Jesus Christ, then you are perfect to not want to be that old sinful man or woman, but at the same time you are not completely free from sin that you and I were born in.

Thanks to Jesus Christ, we will be completely perfect when Jesus comes back again to give us a perfect body and take us to heaven to live with perfect angels and a perfect God.

God created Adam and Eve perfect before they sinned against him.

Their sins caused everything in this world to become imperfect, but Jesus will make this world perfect again because He will burn up all sin in fire and brimstone one day.

The Church is Not Perfect

If you give your life to Jesus, you will not join a perfect church.

If you give your life to Jesus, you will not get baptized in a perfect church.

Many people will get the idea that the church is perfect and is filled with perfect people, but the church is for sinners to be saved in Jesus Christ.

Many pastors will say that the church is like a hospital for sick sinners who need to be spiritually healed by Jesus.

Many people leave the church because their expectations are too high and they expect other people to never make any mistakes in the church.

Many people come into the church and believe that nothing can ever go wrong, but everybody in the church is not rooted and grounded in Jesus Christ.

Even though the church is not perfect, the church is the best place to assemble ourselves and be together to worship Jesus Christ.

The church is not perfect, but as long as we keep going to church we will grow stronger in the Lord because Jesus is the head of the church body and gives us His holy spirit to lead and guide us into all truth of His holy word.

The church is not perfect and we need to keep our eyes on the head of the church, Jesus Christ, who is perfect to have no sins.

The Lord winks his eye at ignorance because he knows that especially a new believer in Him may easily get discouraged when seeing some things not being right in the church.

New believers in Jesus Christ are not on a high spiritual level to understand that nobody in the church is word perfect and action perfect.

New believers in Jesus Christ may not understand that growing stronger in the Lord is a lifetime process.

The church is not perfect, but it's the best place to go to for our faith to grow in Jesus Christ.

Going Through the Great Tribulation

Going through the great tribulation will be very far from being easy, even if you and I know the bible scriptures.

One day, there will be troubled times in this world like it has never seen before and even the strongest and most bible knowledgeable Christians will feel the devil's most intense evil presence all around them.

There are Christians who believe that just because they know the bible scriptures very well, it will be easy for them to go through the great tribulation.

All of the Christians who are alive won't know if they will be strong enough to make it through the worst kind of troubled times, even though they will be sealed in Jesus Christ, who will get them through the great tribulation.

The Lord will put a lot of Christians to sleep and even many children, who the Lord knows won't be strong enough to go through the great tribulation.

You and I can easily believe that we will be prepared to go through the great troubled times, but only the Lord knows if you and I will be fully prepared in our minds and bodies.

The great tribulation will be so bad that even those who are sealed in the Lord won't surely know if they are saved in the Lord Jesus Christ.

It's always good to know the scriptures, especially when the great tribulation comes upon the true Sabbath keepers who will pray to Jesus like they've never prayed before.

Even though they will be sealed in Jesus, they will not truly know it because there will be so much evil around them.

Right now, there are Christians who are going through some tribulation in some places around the world, but the great tribulation will be all around the world before Jesus Christ comes back again.

All the wicked will go through a lot more worse times when God brings his plagues upon them before Jesus comes back again.

Even worse than that, all the wicked will burn up in fire and brimstone in the second resurrection.

A Real Man and a Real Woman

A real man and a real woman will love and obey Jesus Christ, who was a real man without sin when He lived here on earth.

Having a Ph.D. degree doesn't make you a real man or real woman.

Having a master's degree doesn't make you a real man or real woman.

Being a state senator doesn't make you a real man or real woman.

Being a judge doesn't make you a real man or real woman.

A real man and a real woman will love Jesus and keep His Commandments.

Flying an aircraft doesn't make you a real man or real woman.

Driving a tractor trailer truck doesn't make you a real man or real woman.

Being a doctor doesn't make you a real man or real woman.

Driving an expensive car doesn't make you a real man or real woman.

Being the president of the United States doesn't make you a real man or real woman.

A real man and a real woman will love Jesus and keep His Commandments.

Being an engineer doesn't make you a real man or real woman.

Being a mechanic doesn't make you a real man or real woman.

Living in a beautiful house doesn't make you a real man or real woman.

Being a parent doesn't make you a real man or real woman.

Being a police officer doesn't make you a real man or real woman.

Being a soldier doesn't make you a real man or real woman.

A real man and a real woman will love Jesus and keep His Commandments.

Being rich doesn't make you a real man or real woman.

Wearing expensive clothes doesn't make you a real man or real woman.

Being a genius doesn't make you a real man or real woman.

Having big muscles doesn't make you a real man or real woman.

Looking good doesn't make you a real man or real woman.

A real man and a real woman will love Jesus Christ and keep His Commandments.

Will Suffer in Some Kind of Way

If we know to do what is right and don't do it, we will suffer in some kind of way for not doing what is right.

We can do things out of our ignorance and suffer in some kind of way, but if we know to do what is right and don't do what is right we will suffer a lot more beyond our ignorance.

We can do what is right and suffer for doing what is right.

We will suffer a lot more for doing wrong things that we know are wrong to do.

It's much better to suffer for doing something good than to suffer for doing something evil.

Many of us have suffered in some kind of way for doing something wrong out of our ignorance.

Many people have suffered a lot more than you and me for doing something wrong that they knew was wrong to do.

If you and I do something wrong out of our ignorance, we have a much greater chance of recovering from our suffering than people who know that they are doing something wrong and don't care to do what is right.

People who know to do what is right and don't do right will suffer a lot more in the long run because the Lord will make sure they will reap what they sow.

Whatever we do, we all will reap what we sow.

But if we know to do right and don't do right, we will suffer in some kind of way that makes us worse off than people who do wrong things out of ignorance and suffer much less.

No one who ever lived and is alive today will suffer more than Jesus suffered for doing right by His heavenly Father, God.

Jesus suffered and died on the cross for our sins and He rose from the grave with victory over death and the grave to give you and me eternal life when He comes back again for all who suffered for His holy name's sake.

It's much better to suffer for doing right by the Lord than to suffer for doing evil things especially if we know that it's evil that God hates and will sooner or later make us reap the evil that we so.

You Can Thank Jesus

If you are a great-great-grandfather, you can thank Jesus for allowing you to be who you are.

If you are a great-great-grandmother, you can thank Jesus for allowing you to be who you are.

If you are a great-grandfather, you can thank Jesus for allowing you to be who you are.

If you are a great-grandmother, you can thank Jesus for allowing you to be who you are.

If you are a grandfather, you can thank Jesus for allowing you to be who you are.

If you are a grandmother, you can thank Jesus for allowing you to be who you are.

If you are a father, you can thank Jesus for allowing you to be who you are.

If you are a mother, you can thank Jesus for allowing you to be who you are.

If you are an uncle, you can thank Jesus for allowing you to be who you are.

If you are an aunt, you can thank Jesus for allowing you to be who you are.

If you are a brother, you can thank Jesus for allowing you to be who you are.

If you are a sister, you can thank Jesus for allowing you to be who you are.

If you are a nephew, you can thank Jesus for allowing you to be who you are.

If you are a niece, you can thank Jesus for allowing you to be who you are.

If Jesus can bless you with more than one title in your blood family, then Jesus can surely bless you with more than one spiritual title in your church family.

Your church family is your eternal family saved in Jesus Christ who we can never thank enough for allowing you and me to be in His spiritual family that will have eternal spiritual family titles in heaven when Jesus comes back again to take us to heaven.

If you are a son, you can thank Jesus for allowing you to be who you are.

If you are a daughter, you can thank Jesus for allowing you to be who you are.

If you are a grandson, you can thank Jesus for allowing you to be who you are.

If you are a granddaughter, you can thank Jesus for allowing you to be who you are.

If you are a great-grandson, you can thank Jesus for allowing you to be who you are.

If you are a great-granddaughter, you can thank Jesus for allowing you to be who you are.

We can go on and on in the family titles that Jesus allowed to stretch out all around the world to connect to you and me who can thank Jesus for our family tree.

We have a spiritual family tree all around the world where we have spiritual kinfolks who believe in Jesus Christ, who we can never thank enough for all that He does for us to save us from our sins.

It's Good to Keep Quiet

It's good to keep quiet if you are not spoken to.

If you see someone talking to someone else and saying some words you know aren't true, then it's best not to interrupt if you don't know how to correct that person.

God knows that person's heart and God winks his eye at people's ignorance, even though someone may mean good and well about what he or she is saying that is not true.

You and I shouldn't be so quick to want to correct someone, especially someone we don't know because we may deeply offend that person and cause them to curse us out or want to hurt us.

It's good to keep quiet if the Lord doesn't put it in your mind to tell the truth to that someone who you heard telling someone else a lie out of their ignorance.

The Lord will give you and me the opportunity to correct someone at the right time in love without offending him or her, especially with the truth of God's holy word.

If you and I don't listen to the Holy Spirit telling us to keep quiet if we are not spoken to, then we will surely regret it for interrupting other people's conversations.

We can learn something from this conversation, whether they are speaking the truth or not.

It's good to keep quiet if you have doubts about saying something to someone who is not talking to you.

If the Lord put it on your mind to say something to someone who is not talking to you, then there will be no room for any hesitation or doubt in your mind to correct that someone with the truth of God's holy word.

We Christians Shouldn't be Too Hard on Ourselves

We Christians shouldn't be too hard on ourselves if we say something wrong.

We Christians shouldn't be too hard on ourselves if we do something wrong.

If we didn't plan to say something wrong, we shouldn't be too hard on ourselves for saying something wrong.

If we didn't plan to do something wrong, we shouldn't be too hard on ourselves for doing something wrong.

No Christian is perfect to never say something wrong.

No Christian is perfect to never do something wrong.

Many people will judge a Christian for saying something wrong.

Many people will judge a Christian for doing something wrong.

We Christians will be put down the most for saying something wrong.

We Christians will be put down the most for doing something wrong.

We Christians are supposed to set the right example for people to talk right.

We Christians are supposed to set the right example for people to live right.

We Christians shouldn't be too hard on ourselves if we make a mistake.

We Christians are not word perfect.

We Christians are not action perfect.

No Christian knows every good and right word to say.

No Christian knows every good and right deed to do.

No Christian is without sin to be completely like Jesus Christ.

We Christians can have a pure heart to not willfully sin against God, but we will fall short of the glory of God because we were born in sin to have a sinful nature.

We true Christians have pure motives and intentions even though we can say something wrong and do something wrong.

We true Christians do not plan to say or do anything that's not in the will of God because we are all about loving Jesus Christ and keeping His Commandments.

We Christians shouldn't be too hard on ourselves if we unintentionally stumble or fall into a sin that we can confess and repent of unto Jesus Christ.

We Christians should never be too hard on ourselves if we make a big mistake for other people to see and then they might believe that we are not a Christian.

Sanctification is a lifetime process for every Christian to be more and more like Jesus whose righteousness makes every Christian life right before God.

We Christians are judged the most by so-called Christians if we say something wrong or do something wrong in their eyesight.

We Christians shouldn't be too hard on ourselves because Jesus is not hard on us, especially if we unintentionally say something or do something wrong.

Jesus knows that we didn't mean to say it or do it.

Jesus knows that we don't make a habit of saying something wrong or doing something wrong.

Jesus knows that we true Christians are all about being like Him every day, regardless of saying something wrong or doing something wrong on the spur of the moment when we didn't plan to do that.

We true Christians know what it means to talk right and do right by our Lord and Savior Jesus Christ, even though we can say something wrong or do something wrong, and we don't make a habit of it.

We Christians should never be too hard on ourselves if we unwillingly sin against the Lord from our ignorance, because we don't know it all and can say or do something that we that we don't have knowledge of.

We all fall short of the glory of God, unlike Jesus who did not fall short when he lived on earth without sin to save us from our sins.

No Christian is without sin and that is why we Christians can be too hard on ourselves if we say something wrong or do something wrong.

We want to be perfect without sin that we were born in, and we need to confess and repent unto Jesus who is the only one who can save us from our sins.

No Christian can save themselves, regardless of saying and doing what is right.

Our righteousness is like filthy rags to God, who is not too hard on anyone being a Christian or not being a Christian because if God was too hard on us for sinning against Him then he would not have sent us His only begotten Son, Jesus Christ, to save us from our sins.

If God was too hard on us for sinning against Him, we would drop dead as soon as we sinned against Him and no one in this world would be alive today because we have all sinned and fallen short of the glory of God.

It's a Miracle

It's a miracle that I am still alive, when death tried to take me to the grave so many times that I've lost count.

It's a miracle that my health is as good as it is today.

It's a miracle that I am doing as well as I am today.

There were times in life when I was drinking alcohol and speeding on the roads.

The Lord showed mercy on me and didn't let me get in an accident.

That is a miracle to me.

There were times in my life when I got sick with the flu.

The Lord showed mercy on me and didn't let me die from the flu.

That is a miracle to me.

There were times in my life when I was at the wrong place at the wrong time.

The Lord showed mercy on me and spared my life from death.

That is a miracle to me.

It's a miracle that I am still alive today and that miracle is from my Lord and Savior Jesus Christ.

I know that I don't deserve to still be alive today because I had once lived my life so recklessly and away from doing the Lord's will.

No one can explain how a miracle works, but we know that a miracle is supernatural and extraordinary beyond our imaginary and normal senses.

The devil can perform illusions, but these are only counterfeits compared to the real, true miracles from the Lord.

It's a miracle that I am still alive today and doing as well as I am, because the Lord's mercy is miraculous over the devil's illusions that are destructive and can't destroy me for being saved in my Lord and Savior Jesus Christ.

Can Add Up to
and Subtract From

Actions can add up to good actions.

Actions can subtract from good actions.

The tongue can add up to a long life.

The tongue can subtract from a long life.

The body can add up to good health.

The body can subtract from good health.

The mind can add up to genius, brilliance and intelligence.

The mind can subtract from genius, brilliance and intelligence.

The heart can add up to loving everybody.

The heart can subtract from loving everybody.

A job can add up to retirement.

A job can subtract from retirement.

A war can add up to victory.

A war can subtract from victory.

A court case can add up to guilty.

A court case can subtract from guilty.

A marriage can add up to always being together.

A marriage can subtract from always being together.

Memories can add up to feeling good.

Memories can subtract from feeling good.

A book can add up to a good book.

A book can subtract from a good book.

A school board can add up to a good resolution.

A school board can subtract from a good resolution.

Life can add up to going to heaven when Jesus Christ comes back again.

Life can subtract from going to heaven when Jesus Christ comes back again.

Will See No Wrong

Many women will see no wrong in dressing seductive.

Many people will see no wrong in fornicating.

Many people will see no wrong in telling lies.

Many people will see no wrong in gossiping.

Many people will see no wrong in talking bad about people.

Many people will see no wrong in eating unhealthy food.

Many people will see no wrong in robbing people.

Many people will see no wrong in killing people.

Many people will see no wrong in not taking a shower.

Many people will see no wrong in not brushing their teeth.

Many people will see no wrong in being prejudiced.

Many people will see no wrong in talking too much.

Many people will see no wrong in being unfaithful to their spouse.

Many people will see no wrong in joking about people.

Many people will see no wrong in hurting people.

Many people will see no wrong in committing adultery.

Many people will see no wrong in being proud.

Many people will see no wrong in being controlling.

Many people will see no wrong in having unnatural affections.

Many people will see no wrong in showing respect of persons.

Many people will see no wrong in being overweight.

Many people will see no wrong in being deceptive.

Many people will see no wrong in being disrespectful.

Many people will see no wrong in being impolite.

Many people will see no wrong in being rude.

Many people will see no wrong in breaking the law.

Many people will see no wrong in not seeing the doctor.

Many people will see no wrong in not going to church.

Many people will see no wrong in not believing in Jesus Christ.

Many people will see no wrong in doing their own will.

Many people will see no wrong in living in their sins.

Many people will see no wrong in not having a relationship with Jesus Christ.

Many people will see no wrong in turning their backs on Jesus.

Many people will see no wrong in not reading the bible.

Many people will see no wrong in doing evil deeds.

Many people will see no wrong in using people.

Many people will see no wrong in abusing children.

Many people will see no wrong in being violent.

Many people will see no wrong in being quick tempered.

Many people will see no wrong in using drugs.

Many people will see no wrong in drinking alcohol.

Many people will see no wrong in smoking cigarettes.

Many people will see no wrong in not confessing and repenting of their sins unto the Lord Jesus Christ.

Many people will see no wrong in holding grudges.

Many people will see no wrong in not getting an education.

Many people will see no wrong in being ignorant.

Many people will see no wrong in being mean.

Many people will see no wrong in not being saved in Jesus Christ.

Many people will see no wrong in being lost in their sins.

It Will Take

It will take some people to go through a bad experience for them to see how they were wrong about what they believed.

It will take some people to go through a bad experience for them to see how they were wrong about what they said.

It will take some people to go through a bad experience for them to see how they were wrong about how they dress.

It will take some people to go through a bad experience for them to see how they were wrong about how they feel.

It will take some people to go through a bad experience for them to see how they were wrong about disagreeing with someone else who was right about what they said.

It will take some people to go through a bad experience for them to see that they need to wise up.

It will take some people to go through a bad experience for them to see how they were wrong for hurting someone else.

It will take some people to go through a bad experience for them to see how they were wrong for talking bad about someone else.

It will take some people to go through a bad experience for them to see how they were wrong for treating someone else bad.

It will take some people to go through a bad experience for them to see how they were wrong for joking about someone else.

It will take some church folks to go through a bad experience for them to see how they were wrong for showing favoritism to certain people in the church.

It will take some church folks to go through a bad experience for them to see that they were wrong for holding grudges against certain people in the church.

It will take some church folks to go through a bad experience for them to see that they were wrong for believing that they are better than someone else in the church.

It will take some church folks to go through a bad experience for them to see that they were wrong for looking down on someone else in the church.

It will take some church folks to go through a bad experience for them to see that they were wrong for causing someone else to stumble.

It will take some church folks to go through a bad experience for them to see that they were wrong for causing someone else to leave the church.

It will take some church folks to go through a bad experience for them to see that they were wrong for causing someone else to sin against the Lord.

It will take some church folks to go through a bad experience for them to see that they were wrong for taking someone else in the wrong way when their motives were pure in the presence of the Lord.

It will take some church folks to go through a bad experience for them to see that they were wrong for doubting the Lord.

It will take some church folks to go through a bad experience for them to see that they were wrong for not waiting on the Lord to work things out for them.

We all have been through some kind of bad experience to see that we were wrong for not putting all of our trust in the Lord.

Real Life is Not Rehearsed

Real life is not rehearsed like making a movie.

Real life is not rehearsed like a TV show.

Real life is not rehearsed like a TV commercial.

Real life is not rehearsed like a church choir.

Real life is not rehearsed like a Broadway show.

Actors must rehearse their scripts to make a movie.

Actors must rehearse their scripts to make a TV show.

Actors must rehearse their scripts to make a TV commercial.

The church choir must rehearse their songs to sing in the choir.

Musicians must rehearse their instruments to play their music in a musical show.

Singers and dancers must rehearse their voice and body movements to perform in a Broadway show.

Actors can rehearse to make a mistake in a movie.

Actors can rehearse to have a flaw in a movie.

Actors can rehearse to have a bad habit in a movie.

Actors can rehearse to be evil in a movie.

Real life is not rehearsed because we don't rehearse to eat food.

Real life is not rehearsed because we don't rehearse to take a shower.

Real life is not rehearsed because we don't rehearse to get in our cars and drive, we just do it.

Besides being an actor, who in their right mind would rehearse to make a mistake?

Besides being an actor, who in their right mind would rehearse a flaw?

Besides being an actor, who in their right mind would rehearse a bad habit?

Besides being an actor, who in their right mind would rehearse to say bad words

Besides being an actor, who in their right mind would rehearse to do evil?

Real life is not rehearsed, because Jesus Christ never rehearsed anything in the presence of anyone when He lived here on earth without sin in his flesh.

Life can't get more real than Jesus, who never had to rehearse what He would say to anyone.

Life can't get more real than Jesus, who never had to rehearse the miracles that He did in the presence of people.

Real life can never be rehearsed to have no errors like a rehearsed movie with every scene looking so perfect and projecting its story to the audience.

What goes on in real life is no rehearsal to make life look perfect like a movie with actors pretending to make the movie look perfect.

Real life is not rehearsed, because we will do good or we will do evil with no thoughts about rehearsing it.

Even After I Mess Things Up

Even after I mess things up, God is still good to me.

Even after I mess things up, God is still merciful to me.

Even after I mess things up, God is still patient with me.

Even after I mess things up, God is still for me.

Even after I mess things up, God still loves me.

Even after I mess things up, God still forgives me.

God is God.

So, no matter how many times you and I mess things up, God can make something good out of what we messed up.

Adam and Eve messed us all up with sin, but God gave us His only begotten Son to save us from our sins.

Even after I mess things up, God is still God to make my life better if I confess and repent of my sins unto His Son, Jesus Christ.

Even after I mess things up, God is still on His holy throne looking down on me from heaven to make me to be His child, regardless of what I messed up.

Even after I mess things up because I am messed up in sin, God is still God to send His Son, Jesus Christ, back to this world to take me to heaven if I am saved in Jesus.

Even after I mess things up, God still has my back to get me out of things I mess up.

You're Supposed to Love Everybody

You're supposed to love everybody, but don't let anybody use you.

You're supposed to love everybody, but don't let anybody put you down.

You're supposed to love everybody, but don't let anybody push you around.

You're supposed to love everybody, but don't let anybody take advantage of you.

You're supposed to love everybody, but don't let anybody cause you to be dishonest.

You're supposed to love everybody, but don't let anybody cause you to stoop down to their level of foolishness.

You're supposed to love everybody, but don't let anybody cause you to lose your dignity.

You're supposed to love everybody, but don't let anybody make you do something wrong.

You're supposed to love everybody, but don't let anybody make you do what you don't want to do.

You're supposed to love everybody, but don't let anybody get between you and your spouse.

You're supposed to love everybody, but don't let anybody get between you and your children.

You're supposed to love everybody, but don't let anybody get between you and Jesus.

You're supposed to love everybody, but don't let anybody cause you to turn your back on Jesus.

You're supposed to love everybody, but don't let anybody cause you to be lost.

You're supposed to love everybody, but don't let anybody cause you to go to hell.

You're supposed to love everybody, but don't let anybody cause you to rebel against God.

You're supposed to love everybody, but don't let anybody cause you to live in sin.

You're supposed to love everybody, but don't let anybody cause you to be like the devil.

Talkers and Listeners

There are talkers and there are listeners.

There are people who love to talk and there are people who love to listen.

If everybody talked a lot, who would listen?

If everybody listened a lot, then who would talk?

No one can talk and listen at the same time.

The Lord has given many people the gift to talk.

The Lord has given many people the gift to listen.

It's much easier to learn things by listening.

There are good talkers and there are bad talkers.

There are good listeners and there are bad listeners.

There is positive talk and there is negative talk.

There is positive listening and there is negative listening.

Talking about Jesus Christ is always good talk.

Talking about Jesus Christ is always positive talk.

Talking about Jesus Christ is always inspirational talk.

To listen to people talking about Jesus is good listening.

To listen to people talking about Jesus is positive listening.

Listening to people who talk about Jesus is inspirational listening.

Jesus talked a lot to His disciples when He lived here on earth without sin.

Jesus listened a lot to His disciples.

Jesus also talked to anyone who He loved.

Jesus also listened to anyone who wanted to talk to Him.

Jesus was always an inspirational talker.

Jesus was always a good listener and gave the right answers to anyone.

No one will ever be a better inspirational talker than Jesus was.

No one will ever be a better inspirational listener than Jesus was.

Jesus is up in heaven where he talks to us through His Holy Spirit.

Jesus is up in heaven where He listens to us through His Holy Spirit taking our prayers up to Him.

There are talkers and there are listeners in this world.

Only Jesus can truly help a talker to become a good listener.

Only Jesus can truly help a listener to become a good talker.

There are talkers and there are listeners, and they both will be truly blessed for representing Jesus Christ to all the world.

Do You Believe in Jesus Christ?

Do you believe in luck or do you believe in Jesus Christ?

Do you believe in money or do you believe in Jesus Christ?

Do you believe in horoscopes or do you believe in Jesus Christ?

Do you believe in technology or do you believe in Jesus Christ?

Do you believe in science or do you believe in Jesus Christ?

Do you believe in nature or do you believe in Jesus Christ?

Do you believe in your spouse or do you believe in Jesus Christ?

Do you believe in your children or do you believe in Jesus Christ?

Do you believe in a boyfriend or do you believe in Jesus Christ?

Do you believe in a girlfriend or do you believe in Jesus Christ?

Do you believe in a house or do you believe in Jesus Christ?

Do you believe in a truck or do you believe in Jesus Christ?

Do you believe in a car or do you believe in Jesus Christ?

Do you believe in a job or do you believe in Jesus Christ?

Do you believe in education or do you believe in Jesus Christ?

Do you believe in talents or do you believe in Jesus Christ?

Do you believe in skills or do you believe in Jesus Christ?

Do you believe in yourself or do you believe in Jesus Christ?

No other belief is greater than believing in Jesus Christ.

No other belief is surer than believing in Jesus Christ.

No other belief is more real than believing in Jesus Christ.

No other belief is more lasting than believing in Jesus Christ.

No other belief is more victorious than believing in Jesus Christ.

No other belief is more beautiful than believing in Jesus Christ.

No other belief is more hopeful than believing in Jesus Christ.

No other belief is more trusting than believing in Jesus Christ.

No other belief is more guaranteed than believing in Jesus Christ.

No other belief is more powerful than believing in Jesus Christ.

No other belief is more truthful than believing in Jesus Christ.

No other belief is clearer than believing in Jesus Christ.

No other belief is purer than believing in Jesus Christ.

No other belief is stronger than believing in Jesus Christ.

Do you believe in Jesus Christ?

Don't Put Off

Don't put off now for later.

Don't put off today for tomorrow.

Don't put off the present for future.

Don't put off kindness for meanness.

Don't put off peace for strife.

Don't put off gentleness for roughness.

Don't put off selflessness for selfishness.

Don't put off wisdom for foolishness.

Don't put off knowledge for ignorance.

Don't put off good for evil.

Don't put off temperance for gluttony.

Don't put off marriage for fornication.

Don't put off education for stupidity.

Don't put off health for immoderate indulgence.

Don't put off common sense for nonsense.

Don't put off giving for greediness.

Don't put off truth for lies.

Don't put off humility for pride.

Don't put off fairness for inequality.

Don't put off respect for rudeness.

Don't put off Jesus Christ for the devil.

Don't put off Jesus Christ for hell.

Don't put off Jesus Christ for eternal death.

Working for the Lord

Working for the Lord is not about getting rich.

Working for the Lord is about being content.

Working for the Lord is not about keeping your blessings to yourself.

Working for the Lord is about sharing your blessings with others

Working for the Lord is not about being in the limelight.

Working for the Lord is about being humble.

Working for the Lord is not about being right all the time.

Working for the Lord is about loving people, even if they say something wrong or do something wrong.

Working for the Lord is not about how many spiritual gifts you have.

Working for the Lord is about reaching out to others to come to the Lord, even if you only have one spiritual gift to reach out to others with.

Working for the Lord is not only helping others who need the Lord.

Working for the Lord is also about helping yourself because you need the Lord too.

Working for the Lord is not only about being focused on your own soul's salvation.

Working for the Lord is about winning souls to be saved in the Lord Jesus Christ.

The Greatest Travel

Many people in this world love to travel to their favorite places.

Many people love to travel to places they've never been before.

Many people will save up their money to travel.

Many people will travel to another city to look for a job.

Many people will travel to another state to buy a new house.

Many people will travel to another country to go on a tour and sightsee.

Many people will travel across the sky in an aircraft.

Many people will travel on the road.

Many people will travel across the ocean.

Many people love to travel all around the world.

There are people who love to travel beyond the sky.

The greatest travel will one day be for all the righteous children of Jesus Christ, who will be our eternal guide to heaven when He comes back again.

If we are saved in Jesus, we will travel with Him, passing by this sinful world.

If we are saved in Jesus, we will travel with Him, passing by the sun and moon.

If we are saved in Jesus, we will travel with Him, passing by the stars.

If we are saved in Jesus, we will travel with Him, passing by the Milky Way.

If we are saved in Jesus, we will travel with Him, passing by the galaxy.

If we are saved in Jesus, we will travel with Him, passing by the black holes.

If we are saved in Jesus, we will travel with Him, passing by other worlds on our way to heaven with Jesus.

Traveling with Jesus will be the greatest travel to make the travel guide in this world to be forever below Jesus' travel guide to heaven.

The greatest travel will one day be for all the holy saints to travel with Jesus and all the angels back to heaven.

We will not get worn out on our way back to heaven.

If we are saved in Jesus Christ, we will one day soon go on the greatest travel with Jesus.

We will travel with Jesus, passing by every universe that is below the highest heaven where we will go to and celebrate our eternal destination.

As we travel through the outer space with Jesus Christ and all the holy angels, Jesus will illuminate the outer space with His glory of eternal light to pass us by all the black holes in the eternal outer space that Jesus created and can travel through any time He wants to.

The greatest travel will one day come to all the children of God to travel with Jesus back to heaven.

We will have a perfect eyesight to see other worlds and endless solar systems that we will pass by with eternal joy on our way back to heaven with Jesus Christ and all His angels.

Many people will travel to other countries that is a great travel to them, astronauts will travel to the moon that is great travel to them, but it's no comparison to traveling with Jesus one day across all the galaxies and other worlds that is very limited to the highest heaven where Jesus will take us to without us getting tired and worn out on our greatest travel.

Many people will travel in airplanes, trains, buses, motorcycles, cars, trucks, SUVs, RVs, and will travel on ships to be great to them, but if we are saved in Jesus we will one day go on the greatest travel to heaven and won't need to use any restrooms or drink any water to feel refreshed on our greatest travel to heaven.

The greatest travel will be no charge from Jesus who forever knows that no amount of money will ever be enough to pay for the greatest travel to heaven.

You and I and all of God's righteous children will have free airfare to travel with Jesus Christ and all the holy angels to heaven when Jesus comes back again on the clouds of glory.

There will be a number of righteous people that no one can count on the greatest travel to heaven one day.

All the airplanes will be of no use to take the place of Jesus, who will charge us no airfare on the greatest travel of our lives changing from mortal to immortality in Jesus Christ who is eternal life.

No airplanes and no spacecrafts can take us to heaven, that only Jesus can do on the greatest travel.

Made in the USA
Middletown, DE
25 July 2023